RESURRECTION MAN

Eoin McNamee

PICADOR USA 🐟 NEW YORK

Also by Eoin McNamee
The Last of Deeds & Love in History

Picador® is a U.S. registered trademark and is used by St. Martin's
Press under license from Pan Books Limited.

Library of Congress Cataloging-in-Publication Data

McNamee, Eoin
    Resurrection man / Eoin McNamee.
        p.   cm.
    ISBN 0-312-14716-3
    1. City and town life—Northern Ireland—Belfast—Fiction.
    2. Criminals—Northern Ireland—Belfast—Fiction. 3. Belfast
    (Northern Ireland)—Fiction.   I. Title.
    PR6063.C63R47   1995   95-21825
                                                        CIP

First published in Great Britain by Picador

First Picador USA Paperback Edition: November 1996
10   9   8   7   6   5   4   3   2   1

Critical Acclaim for *Resurrection Man* by Eoin McNamee

"Like great film noir, McNamee's dead-on dialogue and elaborate landscapes of memory and violence will stay with you long after the lights go up."
>—L. C. Smith, *Spin* magazine

"An artfully executed tale...a lyrical account of a man in 'pain because of life.'"
>—Olivia Tracey, *The New York Times Book Review*

"Fierce and haunting...Intensity and drive...propel the writing."
>—Paul Skenazy, *San Francisco Examiner & Chronicle*

"McNamee...offers prose that often rises to poetry.... [His] poetic use of geography gracefully establishes the tenseness of everyday life. *Resurrection Man* is a highly compelling read—a beautiful book about ugliness."
>—*San Francisco Review of Books*

"Glorious...McNamee cruises troubled Belfast on the back of a dark angel.... What the reader takes away from this scarifying beauty of a novel isn't so much its body count as its baleful poetry."
>—John Domini, *The Sunday Oregonian*

"With bite and brilliance, rising Irish star McNamee burrows deep.... Eerie, memorable...a chilling first-rate debut..."
>—*Kirkus Reviews* (starred review)

"Intense mastery of rhythm and image...remarkable for its poetic evocations of violence...This book is a chilling masterpiece and a brilliant debut."
>—*Publishers Weekly* (boxed review)

"This is something special.... An extraordinary book."
>—Victoria Glendinning

part one

one

Afterwards Dorcas would admit without shame that having moved house so often was a disturbance to Victor's childhood. But a suspicion would arise in each place that they were Catholics masquerading as Protestants. Her husband James was no help in this regard. He was so backward and shy he needed to stand up twice before he cast a shadow. Dorcas would maintain that Victor did not learn bigotry at her knee even though she herself had little tolerance of the Roman persuasion. She believed that all he really wanted to be was a mature and responsible member of society, loyal to the crown and devoted to his mother. But he suffered from incomprehension. He was in pain because of life.

Dorcas and James came from Sailortown in the dock area. Sailortown disappeared gradually after the war. There is a dual carriageway running through the area now. There isn't even a place where you can stand to watch the traffic. You'd have to get up on a warehouse roof where you might find a lone sniper at dawn, feeling rigorous in the cold and thinking about migration as he watches the traffic, a movement along chosen routes.

The city itself has withdrawn into its placenames. Palestine Street. Balaklava Street. The names of captured ports, lost battles, forgotten outposts held against inner darkness. There is a sense of collapsed trade and accumulate decline.

In its names alone the city holds commerce with itself, a furtive levying of tariffs in the shadow.

James was a dock labourer. He had this deadpan look, a listener to distant jokes. It was like he saw himself as some hardluck figure for whom silence was a condition of survival. Bearing the name of Kelly meant that he was always suspected of being a Catholic. He protected himself by effacement. He was a quiet accomplice to the years of his fatherhood and left no detectable trace.

Sometimes if Dorcas insisted he would take his own son to Linfield matches at Windsor Park. He would get excited and shout at the team. Come on the blues. Victor would look at him then but he would have put the shout away like it was something he'd sneaked on to the terraces under his coat and was afraid to use again.

Once he took Victor up to the projection room during the matinee at the Apollo cinema on the Shankill Road. The projectionist was Chalky White who had been to school with James. Chalky was six feet tall, stooped, with carbon residue from the lamps in his hair and his moustache. There were two big Peerless projectors with asbestos chimneys leading into the ceiling. There were aluminium film canisters on the floor and long Bakelite fuseboxes on the wall. The air smelt of phosphorous, chemical fire.

Chalky showed Victor a long white scar on his arm where he had accidentally touched the hot casing.

'Laid it open to the bone,' Chalky said. He showed Victor the slit in the wall where the projectionist could watch the picture. He talked about film stars he admired. Marion Nixon, Olive Brook. Victor liked Edward G. Robinson and James Cagney in *Public Enemy*. When he looked through the slit he could see Laurence Tierney as John Dillinger laid out on a morgue slab like a specimen of extinction. Flash bulbs went off. A woman said I thought he'd be better looking. Dillinger kept his eyes open, looking beyond the women and the reporters towards his Dakota birthplace, small farms glistening under a siege moon.

James had a photograph of his own father which he kept in his wallet. He was standing with other men in his shift at the docks. They were leaning on their shovels, smoking and stroking their long moustaches like some grim interim government of the dead.

Sometimes when he was watching TV Victor would think he saw his father in the crowd that collected around a scene of disaster. Or standing slightly apart at some great event. Or on the terraces watching great Linfield teams of the fifties and sixties pulling deep crosses back from the byline, scoring penalties in the rain.

After the Apollo Victor worked hard at getting the gangster walk right. It was a combination of lethal movements and unexpected half-looks. An awareness of G-men. During the day he would mitch school and go down to the docks. He would avoid the whores at the dock gate. Their blondie hair they got from a bottle, Dorcas said, and the hair waved in his dreams like a field of terrifying wheat.

Victor spent most of these days behind the wheel of an old Ford Zephyr on blocks at the edge of the dock. The engine had been removed and there was oily grass growing through the wheel arches. It had dangerous-looking fins on the back and chrome bumpers which Victor polished. From the front seat he could see the tarred roofs of goods wagons in the stockyard sidings. Dorcas' brother worked there in a cattle exporter's office. He would sit at their fire at night and talk about cattle, which Victor hated. He had a passion for his work: the bills of lading, statistics of weight loss during transit, mortality rates.

One night when he thought Victor wasn't listening he told Dorcas about finding a Catholic girl in the shed used for storing salt. It was during the thirties. Winter. The wagons were frozen to the rails. The air itself had forceps. The girl and the baby had died in the salt shed with the steam of her labour above her head and the cord uncut between her thighs. When they found her they sliced the cord with the blade of a shovel. When they lifted her they saw salt crystals stuck to her thighs like some geodic shift quarried for her in the moment of her death.

Victor sat at the wheel of the car until dusk most nights. He preferred it when it began to get dark. By day the city seemed ancient and ambiguous. Its power was dissipated by exposure to daylight. It looked derelict and colonial. There was a sense of curfew, produce rotting in the market-place. At night it described itself by its lights, defining streets like a code of destinations. Victor would sit with the big wheel of the Zephyr pressed against his chest and think about John Dillinger's face seen through a windscreen at night, looking pinched by rain and the deceit of women.

It was dusk when Trevor Garrity and Alan McAtee from school found Victor in the car. Garrity sprang the bootlid and looked inside. McAtee went to the driver's window and looked in. Victor had a sense of frontiers, a passport opened to the raw, betrayed face of your younger self.

'How's Pat?' McAtee said. He was three years older and had bad teeth which Victor couldn't stand.

'My name's Victor. Pat's a Taig name.' He wondered how Edward G. Robinson would handle this. Later he would realize that men had been doing this for centuries, stopping each other in remote places, demanding the credentials of race and nationality.

'Kelly sounds like a Taig name to me,' McAtee said casually. 'Your ma must of rid a Taig.'

'Come here till you see this,' Garrity said. McAtee went to the back of the car. Victor followed him. He kept most of his private possessions in the boot and Garrity had emptied them all out onto the ground. There was a scout knife with a fake wooden handle. Twenty Gallagher's blues with a box of matches from the Rotterdam bar. A Smirnoff bottle opener. A copy of *Intimate Secrets Incorporating Married Woman* that Victor had found. When he heard Garrity at the boot Victor expected to lose something. The cigarettes. The knife. Instead he saw that Garrity had the magazine.

'Come here till you see this,' Garrity repeated. McAtee stood beside him and began to read over his shoulder.

'Fuck me, my hubby couldn't believe . . .'

'His wicked love potion drove me . . .'

'I felt a shudder through my most private zone . . .'

'My secret Taig lover by Mrs Dorcas Kelly.'

Victor reached for the knife on the ground. McAtee put his foot on it.

'Pat didn't like that.'

'Pat's sensitive about his ma.'

Victor waited. He could see the shapes of violence laid out in his head like a police diagram with skid marks leading away.

He learned that there was a pattern to such moments. A framework of inconsequential detail. When he took the first blow on the side of the head and went down he was thinking about the last moments of gangsters. He had a sudden awareness of texture and temperature. He understood about people talking about the weather at funerals. He imagined being a gangster and seeing a cockroach or a metal fire escape or something else they had in America. Garrity kicked him in the crotch. A shudder most private. The magazine lay open on the ground beside his head. The Wife of the Month had long yellow breasts, half-hidden, which she seemed to offer in consolation. Her mouth was open as if she was about to utter mysteries, messages of explicit loneliness directed at him. Must of rid a Taig.

They moved to so many districts it didn't seem to matter what Dorcas thought. To rear a son in such a selection of streets did not donate stability to his life; however, she did her best. Victor always took up with older boys, men sometimes, who were not concerned about his moral welfare. He was always in trouble, and she possessed no means to stop it. She thought it was a wonder how she managed to survive this life at all. Pregnant at age seventeen and having to marry in such haste she could barely walk up the aisle with dignity. She thought sometimes she might have married a shadow or a ghost, James was so quiet. She did her duty by him, although there were times she felt an awful emptiness of regret. It was necessary to have firm beliefs to get by. She remembered that Victor wrote to her often of his childhood when he was in prison, always starting his letters 'dear mother' and ending 'yr loving son'.

By age twelve Victor was in trouble for larceny and shop-breaking, led down that path by his elders. She talked to the magistrate with spirit and he got the benefit of the Probation Act that time. James his father never came near the court. She accepted nothing from Victor that was not got honest, and he was always there with small gifts, which is why she wondered at the newspapers — sometimes they printed such lies.

Victor later befriended Garrity and McAtee. He showed them how you could take bus passes off younger pupils and sell them on. Victor would stop someone at the school gate. McAtee would hold them and Garrity would beat them. Victor watched the eyes. It was a question of waiting for a certain expression. You directed a victim towards gratitude. You expected him to acknowledge the lesson in power.

People learned to be obsequious, to defer to him. This led to problems of isolation. He believed he knew how Elvis felt.

After school he would walk down to University Street where he would wait for the Methody girls to come out wearing the compulsory black stockings and high-heeled shoes. They took lessons in deportment, sexual gravitas. Their skirts were worn an inch above the knee and stocking seams were checked with a steel ruler for straightness. They took make-up classes where they learned how to obscure vital faults and arouse precise longings. They were deeply aware of their own attractions. They knew how to prolong moments of anticipation. Lace brassières were visible.

Their fathers would gather in University Street to drive them to their homes outside the city. They performed this task unsmilingly. They avoided looking at the legs of their daughters' classmates and greeted each other with stern nods only. They possessed their daughters as if they were branches of obscure knowledge. There were things that were penetrable only to fathers of beautiful girls, exclusive sorrows.

Afterwards he would go down to the Cornmarket to listen to the preachers and their recital of sectarian histories. They were thin men dressed in black with ravaged faces. They predicted famine and spoke in tongues. Their eyes seemed displaced in time. They would eat sparsely, sleep on boards, dream in monochrome. There was a network of small congregations and merciless theologies throughout the city. Congregations of the wrathful. Baptist. Free Presbyterian, Lutheran, Wesleyan, Church of Latter-day Saints, Seventh Day Adventists, Quakerism, Covenanters, Salvationists, Buchmanites. Pentecostalists. Tin gospel halls on the edges of the shipyard were booked by visiting preachers for months in advance. Bible texts were carefully painted on gable walls.

Victor listened to their talk of Catholics. The whore of Rome. There were barbarous rites, martyrs racked in pain. The Pope's cells were plastered with the gore of delicate Protestant women. Catholics were plotters, heretics, casual betrayers.

When he went home he would find his father washing in the kitchen and Dorcas watching television. *This Is Your Life*. Dorcas would ask where he had been.

'Down at the Cornmarket.'

'Them preachers. In America they have them preachers on the television.' His father walked in, drying his neck.

'You'd better mind yourself, Victor. End up saved, so you will,' he said.

Victor and Dorcas turned to look at each other. James stared over their heads at the television, his inattention cancelling the spoken word.

'Did you hear something?' Dorcas asked Victor.

'Never heard a thing, ma.'

James opened the back door and went out. He kept pigeons at the back. Dorcas said he spent more time with the pigeons than he did with his own family. He never even spent time watching television with them, but moved from one region of silence to another.

'Your da has me tortured,' she said.

'Never mind, ma,' Victor said. 'That guy ain't going to do nothing to you, dollface.' Dorcas laughed.

'Me and yous going to fill that guy full of lead, blow this town.'

Dorcas loved it when Victor talked like this big gangster from the films, but there were times when she would discipline him with a stick in the yard. She remembered that she would be beating Victor and James would cross the yard as if they were not there. Sometimes she thought that what her husband had was a kind of madness. Later Victor read books on it in the Crumlin Road prison, and told her about the different forms of mental absence.

She worried about Victor when she read the letters about madness. They included words that she could not pronounce. Long words whose meaning could only be measured with the aid of finely calibrated and lethally expensive instruments. She could not imagine the consequences of such words. Psycho-pathology. She wondered if such words were dangerous to Victor.

In 1969 the streets began to come alive for Victor. They appeared in the mouths of newsreaders, obscure and menacing, like the capitals of extinct civilizations. Delphi Avenue. He got a delivery job driving a lorry. During the day he would memorize a street, the derelict sites, no right turns, areas strangely compassionate under street-lights. He'd listen to the BBC in the cab. Unity Flats, Kashmir Road. The names took on an air of broken glass, bullet holes circled by chalk, burnt timber doused by rain. He felt the city become a diagram of violence centred about him. Victor got a grip on the names.

On his day off Victor would go down to Crumlin Road magistrates' court. Park the car and then go in, women looking at him. It was a gift he had. Detectives would nod at him in the foyer. Looking good, Victor. It was the quiet respect of the interrogation room, the promise of darker days ahead. Victor sat in the public gallery beside the relatives as the defendants were called in. He liked to see a Taig brought into the box, a man's thin figure wearing a cheap leather jacket and a V-neck jumper. He hated the Taig women sitting beside him. Their anxious looks which he despised. Their air of somebody sitting on a cardboard suitcase on a deserted railway platform, in flight from one half-starved city to another.

He drank in the details of a crime, in particular the ornate details of route and destination. He studied the type of weapon used, barrel rifling and trajectory. The pathologist's report with photographs of entry and exit wounds was handed round the court and he followed its intimate passage from hand to hand.

Lastly there was the testimony of witnesses: I just seen these blue flashes in his hand and the deceased just kind of sat down, I can't explain it. The testimony of detectives from Delta or Charlie division. The kind of look they put on for the judge made Victor laugh. Like, I'm haunted by dates of civil unrest, your honour.

Victor could have any woman he wanted. Click his fingers. But the women only lasted one or two nights. They'd look into his face when they were alone with him and get frightened. Looking into Victor's blue eyes when you were fucking was like watching a televised account of your own death, a disconsolate epic.

He reckoned that Heather was the only woman who ever understood the depth of his ambition. He would always go back to her during the good years. Besides, Victor liked a woman with meat, pockets of flesh you could put your hand into. Towards the end she'd drink Bacardi and cry like hell itself. But at the start it was all Jesus, Victor, I could eat you with salt. Her big slow voice. Come on, you big fucker. I'm dying for a fuck. Take you home and fuck you bendy.

Dorcas said that Victor's favourite programme was Harry Worth. He'd split his sides laughing, she thought he'd burst a vessel. He was always crackers about cars also. His first was a Mk II Escort with wide wheels and this hand you stuck in the back window that waved hello. Big Ivan thought that was the cat's pyjamas. Him and Big Ivan would go down to the car park on the Annadale Embankment, do handbrakes in the gravel.

Before he formed his own unit Victor sat in on several killings. In one they picked up a Catholic on the Springfield Road in a hijacked black taxi. He got a bit of a digging in the back and was moaning by the time they got him to a lock-up garage off the Shankill. They carried him inside. There was an acetylene torch in the corner of the garage. A battery leaked acid on to the floor. Victor wore a blue boiler suit and carried a shortblade knife that he'd got in the Army and Navy stores. There was a smell of butane in the air, a sense of limits reached.

The body was found in a shop doorway on Berlin Street. There were 124 careful knife wounds on the body. Death was due to slow strangulation. The victim appeared to have been suspended from a beam while he was being stabbed. The taxi was found abandoned on waste ground. There were traces of blood on the windows and a woman's lipstick under the passenger seat.

two

There was a cellophane-wrapped ordnance map of the city above Ryan's desk in the newspaper office. He spent hours in front of it. Locations of sectarian assassinations were indicated by red circles. Many of these represented call-outs, the phone ringing late at night and a drive across the city through checkpoints. He would reach the place in driving rain. There would be a scene-of-crime officer, fingerprint and forensic men. The forensic men had fine hair and glasses. They wore white boilersuits and rarely spoke. They approached a corpse with gravity, removing it to another context.

There were lines on the map too, indicating rivers, areas which had been demolished, suggested escape routes following a bomb, zones of conflict, boundaries, divisions within the heart. Ryan drew a new one on the map almost every day. An evolution had been going on in there over the past three years, a withdrawing behind the lines. He thought he could learn something by keeping a record of encroachments and retreats. He was trying to develop the knowledge that the inhabitants of the city had. The sense of territory that guided them through hundreds of streets. That feeling for the anxious shift in population. He stared at the lines and circles that proposed something beyond the capacity of maps. His markings were like the structure of a language. He expected to hear its guttural sound being pronounced on the streets. He imagined being addressed in it. It would be arcane, full of sorrow, menacing.

Ryan had been working with Ivor Coppinger for two years. Coppinger was more deeply involved. It was Coppinger for instance who conducted meetings in parked cars with off-duty police and UDR men. There were intricate relationships involved once the contact was made. Knowledge became a form of suffering. In the end the information became almost incidental. Coppinger listened to terrible things about ambition, parenthood.

Early that morning he had gone with Coppinger to the Albert Bridge. A chemical tanker had been parked on the bridge with a bomb on board. He got to the scene just as the area was being sealed off. They were waiting for someone from the fire brigade to identify the cargo. The lorry was on the pavement with its hazard warning lights on. The man from the fire brigade could not read the cargo labels without binoculars. While someone went for them they stared at the orange decals at the back of the tank, symbols of mass panic and death by inhalation. The bomb disposal men were moving slowly up the Albert Bridge Road, pausing at intervals as if they were aware of other signs, not easily detectable: a shift in the breeze, a magnetic tug of warning in the currents of the Lagan beneath the bridge. Before they reached the lorry the detonator had gone off without piercing the tank. The man from the fire brigade said afterwards that it contained dry-cleaning fluid.

Coppinger had told him about Constable McMinn and Frames McCrea. McCrea had crashed through 164 checkpoints in stolen cars. McMinn had been picked to catch him because he was a part-time rally driver. There was a network on the outskirts of the city to which he belonged. Sullen men working in garages, stripping engines on oil-soaked benches, grinding down valves, increasing ratios, moving towards devout moments of speed and power. Small local papers carried intense motor-sports coverage, photographs of morose champions.

McCrea had become a matter of legend. He was at the centre of mystical events. The cars he stole had been peppered with bullets. He had jumped a checkpoint ramp and landed on the Stockman's Lane motorway access. He stopped outside Tennant Street RUC station every night and held the horn down to provoke a chase.

When McMinn rammed him off the road in Amelia Street the reaction was extreme. Two nights ago McMinn and his partner were dragged into the Victoria bar. They were forced to crawl on their hands and knees. They had to walk like chickens. McMinn was taken into the toilets where a shot was fired into the wall beside his head. He was forced to eat shit.

Coppinger pointed this out as an indication of the feelings aroused. The deeply felt immunities of the hero had been breached.

That afternoon Coppinger put the medical report of the first knife killing on Ryan's desk. After death the head had been almost severed from the trunk. There were two depressed fractures of the skull, fragments of glass embedded in the face. The root of the tongue had been severed.

Later that afternoon Ryan drove Coppinger out to the scene.

'They would've parked the car there,' Coppinger said, pointing to the mouth of a small alley.

'Drag marks,' Ryan said, examining the pavement. There were bloodstains against the wall. There was nothing to distinguish the bloodstains or the doorway where the body had been left, but they both had a sense of familiarity, of scenes repeated in history.

'They would have done your man out of view in the alley,' Coppinger said, his finger describing their progress, 'dead or near enough.'

'He was strangled, cut to pieces.'

'I reckon they kept him alive though, until they got here. They wanted him to know who was doing it.'

Ryan followed Coppinger's thinking. The point of a random sectarian killing was its randomness, but here the killer wanted to be known to the victim. He wanted to convey familiarity. The cry of the victim as a form of address. The killer would demand ritual. He would sever the throat regardless of arterial blood. He would hold the knife aloft.

Ryan found himself thinking about the way Margaret used to mutter in her sleep at night. She would mention unironed shirts, a room which needed wallpaper. Interior conversations composed of oceanic trivia which left him feeling sleepless and adrift.

'The head was attached to the body by tissue at the back,' Coppinger said. 'It near fell off when he was moved.'

There was a certain awe in his tone. There was someone out there operating in a new context. They were being lifted into unknown areas, deep pathologies. Was the cortex severed? They both felt a silence beginning to spread from this one. They would have to rethink procedures. The root of the tongue had been severed. New languages would have to be invented.

three

Heather waited for Darkie Larche in the top room of the Gibraltar bar. There was sunlight coming in through the dusty windows and she put her legs on a pile of pamphlets to catch it. She loved the sun like life itself. Any chance she got she'd smear herself in oil and sit out in the Ormeau Park like some Buddha you saw in a book. She felt a voracious tenderness in the sun. She dreamed of beaches in Spain, high-rise hotels, oiled bodies that gave you the daytime sadness you felt for those who died young. Children with wasting diseases, teen-age girls in car crashes.

The television was on in the corner with the volume turned down. She wasn't like the other women who came into the bar, watching every news they could in case their street would appear. They looked on TV like a navigation system, migrating home through the channels. She watched scenes of street violence with the volume turned down. It gave her a sense of survival that she liked. Darkie called it the body count and watched it to check on incidents that his unit had been involved in. He would shake his head in sorrow at inaccurate details; a victim's age given wrongly. It implied a lack of respect, an improper observance of the formalities. It was somehow vital to him that a victim's age, religion and the exact location of the hit be given precisely. Errors were subversive. They denied sectarian and geographic certainties.

The room was filled with metal filing cabinets and unopened piles of literature. It was Heather's job to ensure that these were distributed. Glossy pamphlets with full-colour pathologist's photographs of bomb victims were sent anonymously to politicians and journalists. The reds and blues of exposed veins and mutilated fatty tissue reminded her of Twelfth bunting. Packing them in envelopes she felt like the organizer of a sad parade.

Other pamphlets were more conventional. For God and Ulster. No Surrender.

Darkie came in, looked at the television and went to the window. He had brown skin and high cheekbones, remnants of a Huguenot merchant ancestry. He was continually nervous with a kind of racial edginess, the dissenter's fear of pogrom. He came over to the desk and flicked at the pile of pamphlets with the tip of a ruler. He moved behind Heather and slipped a hand into the opening of her blouse, fingering her breast as if he had come across a mislaid object. Heather had often come across this kind of sexual absentmindedness in members of various organizations. And she remembered it in two young British intelligence officers she had met at a party the week before. Soft-eyed boys with north-country accents who disappeared together into a back bedroom as soon as they arrived, then stood around shyly afterwards, their trembling lips a little open as if they were on the verge of making secret disclosures, revelations of fellatio.

'Take your blouse off,' Darkie said, keeping his eyes on the television. She felt him shift his grip and remained still. 'This fucking Victor Kelly character has that lot downstairs in fucking palpitations. Take your blouse off.'

'Make me. Who's Victor Kelly?'

'This character hangs round the Pot Luck with Big Ivan Crommie and Willie Lambe. Thinks he's God's gift to the movement. Word is his da's a Catholic. Thinks he's some kind of hard man. Shooting the mouth off about how the only way to do someone is with a knife, for fuck's sake. Take it off or I'll rip it.'

'Take her easy, Darkie, it's only new. So what's the citizens' army so worried about?'

'Don't be so fucking sarcastic. They're all scared out of their shite of him for some reason. My fucking granny's ninety, has palpitations if she wins ten bob at the bingo. This lot's supposed to be a unit. Defenders of the faith and all. Are you going asleep on me or what?'

'What's your big mad rush anyhow?'

'Supposed to be a council meeting at six. Look very professional, so it would, them walking in and me sticking it in for God and for Ulster. Look at them bastard politicians on the TV – us down here doing their dirty work for them.'

'If you're going to do it, do it right. It's not a fire you're poking.'

'Say it was him that cut this poor fucking Taig to pieces with this knife. Boy they found on Berlin Street.'

'Who did – put your hand there.'

'Victor Kelly, I told you. My granny . . .'

'What?'

'I says my granny . . .'

'Fuck your granny.'

She liked Darkie. He was sensitive to the pain his organization inflicted. He watched funerals on the news, commented on the age of the children following the cortège. He had a sense of obligation. He was committed to a wider vocabulary of death which included widows and children. She liked his inattention, his slim brown cock, his seriousness.

She left him in the office and went downstairs where she ordered a Bacardi at the bar. There was still sunlight coming through the windows and the sandbagged doorway. Late after-noon. The sound of traffic. City centre office workers dispersing to their homes on the outskirts with the radio turned up high for news of diversions, checkpoints in the radial suburbs.

The barman had to say her name several times before she took her change. It was a quality in her that women disliked. A lack of focus. A physical memory dwelt on.

There were four or five men in the corner of the bar talking about guns.

'I could get you this Lee-Enfield. Perfect nick. Come across in the *Claudia*.' The *Claudia*. The turn of the century arms smuggler, a potent name riding in the offshore currents of an empire's memory. Source of arms, blockade runner, succourer of outposts.

'Lee-Enfield my arse. Tell us this, how do you hide a rifle in a fucking crowd? The pistol's your only man. The revolver. Smith and Wesson.'

'Browning.'

'Fucking Magnum.'

One of the men detached himself from the group, joined his hands and arched his back. The others stopped talking and watched. He straddled an imaginary victim lying on the ground.

'This way you see into his eyes.'

He lowered his joined hands until they were within a foot of the ground and moved as if from recoil.

'Keep looking in the eyes. Boom. Fucking brains out.' The man lifted the front of his shirt and mimed pushing a weapon into his waistband, then stepped back to the bar and lifted his drink.

'That's fucking all right close up. What happens you want to plug the bastard from the roof. Out a window?'

'That takes your SLR, your Armalite, your Kalashnikov.'

'Not the fucking Lee-Enfield's been sitting in your ma's attic this past fifty years getting blocked up with mouseshit.'

They were appreciative of the mechanisms of death. Some of them were ex-soldiers and had travelled to places such as Cyprus, Belize. Their sentences had a dusty, travelled air, a patina of hillside ambushes and jungle airlifts that the others respected. They wore highly polished shoes and saluted with pride at the cenotaph on Remembrance Sunday. On Saturday morning at dawn they took groups of men outside the city for small-arms training.

They cultivated the carefully selected victim, economy of movement, the well-aimed single shot to the head. They were in control of their hatred. It was a tactical asset. They were worried about the young men coming into the organization and their dependence on random structures.

Over the following year most of them were interned on the HMS *Maidstone* moored in the lough, or in the prefabs of Long Kesh. They accepted this, lived by army discipline and spent their days constructing a rueful politics, things that prisoners work at alone in their cells, improvising in solitude.

Heather had slept with one of them when she first came to the city. He had taught her some Malaysian words in the bar. The word for where. The word for how much. She spoke them to him in the back seat of his car. She imagined him in a foreign brothel pointing to her. I'll take that one. Leading her upstairs. The laughter from other rooms. The malarial silences.

She had been brought up in a seaside town twenty miles from the city. There was a network of these towns stretching along the coast from the city. During the summer people from the city stayed in guest-houses and littered the dunes with bottles and sandwich wrappers. Their arrival each bank holiday was momentous, a movement of populations. A desperate trek with ten-mile tailbacks. Sacrifices were being made, hardships endured.

In winter the town was empty, sand blowing in the car parks. She went drinking in the dunes with hollow-eyed local boys. The front was deserted. She liked walking there, inventing reasons why there was no one in the town any more. She imagined herself the sole survivor of an epidemic, a vast contamination of loneliness. Clouds massed along the skyline. Tidal surges left large boulders on the breakwater and driftwood in the outdoor swimming pool on the promenade. Walking on the front she could feel the sea grinding against the concrete beneath her feet. She tried to decipher voices in the sea. She thought she could detect a vocabulary of forces. At home she listened to the shipping bulletins, lying in bed at night with a transistor beside her, stations inching their way off the air with mariners' jargon.

She moved to the city at eighteen and worked in bars. She began to move towards the loyalist pubs. The Pot Luck, Maxies, the Gilbraltar. Men smiled at her. Hey, big tits. She took a flat above a Chinese restaurant and beside a hairdresser's on the Lisburn road. The smell of perming lotion leaked through the floorboards and walls. In the evening Chinese men played cards in the yard of the take-away surrounded by chickens in plastic freezer bags. They talked softly to each other in Chinese, a rivertongue of strange gamblers she felt familiar with. She would lean on the window-sill listening to them, voices in a dim light, a vernacular darkness which seemed lit by the yellow chickens defrosting in trays.

Ryan rang the police press office to confirm the details of the Berlin Street killing. They said they had no details. Cause of death to be established. A language of denial was being employed. His editor refused to accept the story without confirmation.

'I saw him in the morgue,' Ryan said. 'He was cut to ribbons.'

'Get confirmation.'

'They won't confirm. They'll wait a year on the inquest finding. His head nearly fell off when they lifted him.'

'Come back to me on it tomorrow.'

'Story's dead tomorrow. It was like he had these long cuts all over his body. Hundreds of them. You could tell he was alive when they cut the throat. A witness says he heard someone saying kill me, please just kill me.'

'OK, write it up.'

The story did not appear in the morning edition. It was not the first time this had happened. Ryan thought he detected a failure of nerve, a reluctance to admit the terrible news.

After work he went to the Europa hotel. It was one of the first places to introduce body searches at the entrance. The hotel was bombed regularly. It had most-bombed-hotel status. Ryan had noticed increased local awareness of the value of such detail. Most-shot-at police station. Contempt was expressed for quiet areas.

Ryan went into the Horseshoe bar and ordered a drink. He watched the foreign correspondents come in. Photographers in khaki shirts with big pockets. Older men in safari jackets who looked continually dazed. It was said they had trouble distinguishing between assignments. One of them had told him that other wars kept creeping into his reports. His memory was swamped with incident. The presidential palace is surrounded. Armed gangs are roaming the commercial sector. There were long silences when he read these reports down the phone to his night editor in London. At a nearby table another group of English journalists was drinking heavily.

'I saw the bomb in Woolworth's today.'

'It's his first bomb.'

'You stand around for hours and then it goes off. The building just collapses silently and then the sound hits you. There's something comic about it.'

'It's a sonic delay. The blast travels faster than the sound. The blast is over by the time the sound gets to you.'

'The fucking building collapses and there's no noise. Then boom. It's like it was staged. Like Buster Keaton was going to walk out of the dust or something.'

'Did you ever smell gelignite. It smells exactly like marzipan. Cake mixture.'

'There was a lot of dust. I never thought of dust. Flames yes.'

'Women in aprons. Orange peel. Glacé cherries.'

*

Coppinger came in and ordered a pint of Bass. He'd been drinking in Tiger Bay. Listening to stories about the Blitz, Kingdom Brunel in Belfast, the construction of the *Titanic* in the shipyard. He said that a cousin of his father's had accidently been sealed in the *Titanic*'s double hull and the body had never been found. It was a haunted ship, he said. There was a ghostly tapping below the waterline.

Ryan followed his gaze towards a small group of men in a corner of the bar. Two of them he recognized as paramilitaries. The other two were unfamiliar but they had a military air about them. They could have been arms dealers. Ex-army steeped in counter-terrorist lore. The effect of rapid fire in an urban warfare situation. Arranging consignments of weapons from Rotterdam warehouses in crates marked machine parts. Kalashnikov. But Coppinger pointed out that the clothes were wrong.

'A quartermaster's notion of what you wear drinking in a hotel bar. Sports jackets, two, tweed. Ties, matching.'

Meetings like this were taking place all over the city. Fields of operations were defined. Documents of safe passage were granted. Information was exchanged. At official level these meetings did not take place. Accusations of army collusion with paramilitary groups were vehemently denied but the army continued to negotiate at ground level. People were aware of levels of duplicity being created. Irrational guilt complexes were being reported by doctors. The level of heart disease and road death was under investigation. Coppinger said he had difficulty in maintaining an erection. Teenage suicide was on the rise.

Ryan's thoughts turned back to the knife murderer. He considered the idea of an evangelist with burning eyes, a seeker after fundamental truths. Stripping away layers with a knife to arrive at valid words. Please. Kill me.

'Place is coming down with pros,' Coppinger said, indicating a fair-haired girl standing at the bar. She saw him and moved towards them. There were freckles between her breasts and her nipples were visible beneath her blouse.

'Your headlights is on,' Coppinger said when she came up beside them.

Ryan thought for a moment about taking her home. He had an urge for feigned desire. He wanted to hear an invented language of sex, its expressions of forgetfulness and terror.

When they left it was raining. The city centre was always empty after five o'clock. Street lighting was sparse as if areas of darkness had been agreed. You got a feeling of single cars cruising the streets with sinister gleams from their windscreens. Drizzle falling from a vigilante sky.

four

Sometimes Victor would take Big Ivan and Willie Lambe on a night-time tour. It was a game he liked to play. He would sit in the back of the car with his eyes closed and tell them where they were. They argued about how he did it. Big Ivan said it was the sense of smell. Bread from the Ormeau bakery, hot solder near the shipyard, the hundred yards stink from the gasworks. Big Ivan reckoned that he mapped the city with smells, moving along them like a surveyor along sightlines. Willie thought of pigeons homing. Migrations moving to some enchanted and magnetic imperative.

Driving in and around the Shankill his recitations became more ambitious. He knew the inhabitants of every house and would tell their histories, give details of women's lives lived on the intricate margins of promiscuity. This was the bit that Willie liked. Victor always had a ride on his arm. He told them about the forty-five-year-old schoolteacher who waited for him dressed as a widow. Or Sawn-off, the sixteen-year-old with inverted nipples. Big Ivan was haunted by this idea. He tried to imagine the nipped ends. It was part of the imagery of women which scared him. Part of hosiery, bra sizes, the language of B-cup, D-cup, something he couldn't cope with. He thought about women's ironic conversations in changing rooms. Terrifying dialogues carried out over the lingerie counter in Anderson and Macauley's department store. Fifteen denier. Sheer.

Sometimes when they stopped the car outside the Pot Luck or Maxies Victor would stay in the back seat, his lips

moving. It was an inventory of the city, a naming of parts. Baden-Powell Street, Centurion Street. Lonely places along the river. Buildings scheduled for demolition. Car parks. Quiet residential areas ideal for assassination. Isolated gospel halls. Textures of brick, rain, memory.

Joining the UVF put him in touch with Big Ivan, Willie and others. Onionhead Graham. Hacksaw McGrath. He learned about serious money. First of all just going into shops and taking things. He learned that he didn't have to threaten. Shopkeepers were glad to hand over goods. He was relieving them of hidden fears, split-second images of wives and children being confronted by masked men. Then he started going on to building sites and offering protection. He believed they would sleep better by paying him. No-warning bombs were frequent. People were being gunned down in the street. He was offering them a place in random events and always made a point of calling at the same time every week. He was the means by which they could align themselves to unpredictable violence.

With his first real money he bought a black Ford Capri from Robinson's showrooms. Robinson gave him the nod when it came in. Here's a 007 for Victor he said, a fucking Bondmobile. He hinted at lethal extras, hidden blades, machine-guns behind the headlights. He was a gifted salesman and knew what Victor wanted. He regarded car showrooms as centres of subliminal knowledge. People lowered their voices instinctively. The lighting was austere and respectful. The cars were tended daily by mechanics in white overalls. He would open the car door and invite the customer to enter the interior with its smell of imitation leather, polish and warm plastic. He wanted them to feel dazed and exalted. He picked out the Capri for Victor because it had suggestions of power and generosity. It implied little margin for error, lives on the edge.

Victor was in Maxies the night they got John McGinn. They

had picked him up earlier on the Crumlin Road. Maxies was to be the Romper Room. The name was taken from a children's television programme where the presenter looked through a magic mirror and saw children sitting at home. You sent in your name and address if you wanted to be seen through the mirror. The magic mirror had no glass. It was thought to contain secrets of longevity. It gave you access to the afterlife.

'What's your name?'

'John.'

'John fucking who?'

'John McGinn.'

'Through the magic mirror today we can see John McGinn. Hello John. We'll call you Johnnie. Do your friends call you Johnnie? We're your friends.'

We share your sense of bewilderment. Your intense lone-liness. You were in a hurry walking down the Crumlin Road. You were going to work, to a night class, to meet a woman in a bar. We can hear her crying because you didn't turn up. We share her sadness. We will be a comfort to her.

'Over to you Victor.'

'Fucking butterfingers.'

'Hey, he near broke my foot. He's got something hard in there.'

'It's his fucking skull.'

'He levitated. I swear to God he levitated over the bar. He's a magician or something.'

'Here's a message for the fucking Pope.'

Billy McClure was the first to use the Romper Room. He was familiar with forms of initiation. He had convictions for paedophilia and knew that complicity was everything. It was a question of maintaining a ceremonial pace with pauses and intervals for reflection. There had to be a big group of partici-pants. Twenty or thirty was good, particularly if they were close-knit. That way you could involve whole communities. You implicated wives and children, unborn generations. The reluc-tant were pressed forward and congratulated afterwards.

'Good man, Billy.'

'I seen teeth coming out. I definitely seen teeth. There's them on the floor over there.'

'You can come around our place give the wife one of them digs any time, Billy.'

There were long pauses for drinking. Men crowded round the bar eager to buy rounds for the whole company. The victim was ignored. He lay on the ground between the poker machine and the pool table. There was blood on the ground, bits of scalp. Victor would wander over with a drink in his hand, stir McGinn with his boot and stare blankly at him as if he were a specimen of extinction.

Later Victor would see that these events had formal structure. The men settled down after the first round of drinks. They took their jackets off and precision became important. A whole range of sounds could be extracted from the victim. The third stage came around 3 a.m. No one spoke. The men's breathing was laboured. It was 3 a.m., hour of mile-deep disappointments. Futility and exhaustion began to set in.

At 4 a.m. Victor took McGinn into the toilets where he cut his throat.

Heather found out later that it was Billy McClure who had suggested the parties in her flat. Heather didn't like McClure. Every time he saw her he gave her this smile and this look. The look made her think of a Bible prophet from Sunday school, their bodies abraded by dust-storms and suffering. The smile made her think of unbearable distances, mindless perspectives. He would arrive at the parties accompanied by four or five silent boys. Skinheads. They wore identical boots, white shirts and Wrangler parallels. They had No 1 haircuts with blue veins visible beneath the stubble like caste marks. They did not drink or smoke. Their seriousness marked them out.

Darkie told her later that McClure's speciality was the mentally handicapped. The body of a retarded fourteen-year-

old marked with hot pokers was found in a quarry on the Black Mountain. He had discovered in them the transcendent possibilities of silent suffering. They did not know how to express pain. He was a member of the Aryan brotherhood and had a roomful of Nazi memorabilia at home. Swastika armbands, SS cap badges, officers' chevrons. He knew the importance of insignia, how they were invested with secret energies and possibilities of transformation. He understood the Nazis' extension of language into power.

At first Heather was against the parties. Darkie explained to her that they were necessary. Various strands had to be brought together, introductions arranged, informal contacts had to be made. She could understand that. It was the fact that McClure was involved that worried her. She suspected that there was another agenda. He was in there from the start, an underlying problem, some kind of deep thematic disturbance she couldn't put her finger on.

'I don't know,' she said. 'It's like McClure, it's like you woke up after this bad dream and you can't remember what it was except that it scared the shit out of you and then you see McClure and you remember.'

She thought that Darkie would laugh when she said that but he just gave this kind of shy grin which worried her.

The morning before the first party Darkie arrived at nine o'clock with a transit van. Heather was in bed and had to get up to let him in.

'What the fuck, Darkie,' she said, 'it's only nine o'clock Saturday morning, girl needs her sleep.'

Darkie slipped his hand quickly into the gap of her dressing gown then went to the van and came back carrying a case of Black Bush whiskey. She had a sudden feeling about the rest of her life. About a man who came to her house every week and touched her breast as if it was necessary to register a palm print against her heart, a password. She looked out and saw crates of beer piled on the pavement.

'We expecting a fucking army or what, Darkie? Is there a

new regiment in town or what? Maybe it's all for me? Maybe this is a message I'm drinking too much or something? Would you mind telling us what you're at?'

Darkie was in the lounge moving furniture to the sides of the room.

'Darkie, this is getting on my tits so it is.'

He was absorbed in engineering the party. Wide open spaces in the middle of the floor, intimate niches near the windows, easy access to the bedroom. He put a framed photograph of her father into a drawer and moved a standard lamp from one corner of the room to another then pulled the curtains to see the effect. Heather felt the room flooded with innuendo.

She was upstairs getting dressed when she heard the doorbell. She looked out of the window and saw a telephone engineers' van parked at the kerb. She heard Darkie opening the door. Minutes later he came in through the bedroom without knocking. There were two men wearing overalls behind him, one of them carrying a box with a khaki telephone attached. They inspected the room as if she wasn't there. One of them then said 'behind the bed' in an English accent.

'Darkie.'

'They're here for the phone is all. Come on with me, get some breakfast. I'm fucking starving so I am.'

The parties were held every Saturday night. Most of the time Heather did not know the people who arrived or how they knew her address. She studied her front door for cryptic marks like in a book. In the end she became accustomed to opening the door to well-spoken Englishmen in suits, off-duty policemen, senior figures in the UDA and faces she recognized from the television. Sometimes there would be men she recognized from the Gibraltar coming in awkwardly like barbarian chiefs from the outlands bringing with them a smell of cooking fires and fresh blood.

The policemen would gather in the kitchen where they talked about guns: rates of fire, target density. Nervous conversations conducted in an edgy dialect of ballistics. They got drunker than anyone else and held quick-draw competitions with side-arms in the hallway.

The Englishmen in suits would wait for the arrival of McClure with the boys. He took the boys into a bedroom and made them wait. A staged delay hinting at complicated preparation. The men fixed each other's ties and began to make small feminine gestures. The group seemed to be strengthened by their shared anticipation so that when McClure came out and waved the first one into the room a murmur of gentle encouragement came from the others. Heather thought they looked like candidates for interview. That McClure and his boys were waiting behind the door to probe them on the significant regrets of their lives, to debrief them of crucial sorrows.

They emerged with their heads down, walking gently as if escorted from the room by some disconsolate presence.

Darkie would go drinking in local discos to bring back new girls. They were always impressed by the cars parked outside the flat. RS2000s, Opel Mantas in rally spec, Escorts with wide wheel arches and magnesium alloy wheels. Things to conjure with. Rich paintwork suggesting the visionary landscape of the showroom catalogue. The UDA men were popular with these women. They carried wads of cash in their hip pockets and played money games with the girls, inserting twenty-pound notes into apertures in their clothing. It was all obvious. Nothing was left to chance. The girls' squeals and gestures of denial were artificial. There were overtones of family violence, red-eyed fathers beating their daughters with belts. Occasionally one of them would move away from a man and smooth her skirt down primly. The man would gaze sullenly into space. A sign that he had left out a detail of the flirtation.

On the third Saturday night a girl did a striptease on the living-room floor. A retired sergeant from the B-Specials used a torch as a spotlight and men tried to pull her on to their knees. Once she had taken her blouse off there was a seriousness to her movements as though she was trying to piece together a precise sequence of arousal from remembered fragments. A boy who held her against the wall and whispered. The smell of rain. She turned away from her audience, her hips moving, unfastening the strap of her white bra. Heather wanted to touch her narrow back, its discovered grace. She thought about words you used when you were young. Promise you won't tell if I let you. I never let nobody before.

Often towards morning Heather would come across one of the Englishmen leaving the bedroom, shivering, and with his eyes blank as though he had just returned from a journey in which he carried the unbearable news of his own death.

Drinking in the Botanic Inn Ryan had a phone call telling him to meet Coppinger in the Gasworks bar on the Ormeau Road. Walking through the University area he detoured through Chlorine Gardens to Stranmillis where he had lived with Margaret. There had been several visiting professors and a television producer living in the same street. There was a small coffee shop where their wives gathered in the morning and Ryan had gone there sometimes to listen to them. Conversations he imagined you would hear at embassy parties in the eastern bloc or foreign compounds in Gulf states. The inadequate grasp of local politics, talk of staff becoming sullen and unco-operative, the belief in the army's ability to maintain order on the streets. There were symptoms of bewilderment and a fear of last-minute evacuation.

The windows of the Gasworks bar were covered with wire mesh. You entered through an unlit corridor of sandbags. Heads turned towards the door when he entered the bar. Ryan felt suspect. There was no sign of Coppinger. As soon as he walked in he knew he was going to be singled out. He had trouble summoning the correct responses. It was a question of assembling an identity out of names: the name of school attended, the name of the street where you lived, your own name. These were the finely tuned instruments of survival. He lurched towards the toilets. Inside he leaned his head against the wall in front of him while he pissed. The sound of running water was deafening, ruinous. He read the word Adamant stamped on the massive Victorian urinal. The name had a monumental quality. It had the strength of great certainties. Cast-iron, porcelain. The men who installed it built bridges, gasworks, canals. They were capable of assessing the quali- ties of a material, its interior conviction, and measuring it against their own. Brass taps, lead pipes. He heard a voice behind him, almost inaudible over the sound of flushing water. He waited to be pushed against the wall and interrogated, realizing it was a mistake to leave the crowded bar for this place which dealt in functional truths, and it was a minute before he recognized Coppinger's voice.

'Fuck's sake, I reckoned you'd be skulking in here scared out of your shite, Ryan, you big girl's blouse you.'

They sat in a corner away from the bar. Coppinger pointed to a sheet of fake wood stuck roughly over the bar.

'There's bullet holes behind that,' he said. 'Fuckers opened fire through the window last month.'

Ryan had noticed people pointing out bullet marks and bomb sites. They added to the attraction of the city. Blood- spots on the pavement were marked by wreaths. Part of a dark and thrilling beauty.

Coppinger was talking about the knife killing. He had been given a list of possible names for those involved. His informant had insisted that he did not write them down. They had to be committed to memory. Coppinger had sat for an hour in a parked car on the Ormeau embankment chanting names until it seemed that the recitation was an end in itself, a means of fathoming the forces at work. As if the knowledge they were looking for was concealed in the names themselves. It seemed possible. It was a clear night. There was mist on the river and the words in his mouth became strange. He could have been naming distant galaxies. He began to detect elemental properties in these words devoid of their associations, the dense tribal histories attached to a name.

'Who was mentioned?'

'Darkie Larche. Onionhead Graham. Mostly Darkie's crew. Problem is something like this isn't Darkie's style.'

'Any idea where they're operating out of?'

'The usual places were mentioned. The Pot Luck. The Gibraltar. Maxies maybe.'

'Anything else?'

'Not a whisper. People's jumpy as fuck on this one. You ring the peelers even and you talk to someone who won't give their name and they pass you on to some other bastard won't give his name and they put you on to the press office who says that investigations is continuing.'

'Are they pursuing a line of enquiry? Are they looking for anyone in particular? The driver of a blue car seen in the vicinity? A woman walking her dog near the scene? A woman walking her dog'd be a good witness. It's something to do with kindness to animals and regular habits.'

'Nothing like that. Nobody round here sees nothing no more. Even a woman walking the dog's looking the other way.'

'Give me some of those names again.'

'Darkie Larche. Onionhead Graham.'

'I don't know, where do they think they are? Chicago in the twenties? Maybe we should be looking for information from the fucking FBI, the fucking Pinkertons. Maybe it's just the police know fuck-all, sounds like they know fuck-all.'

'It's like everybody's frightened, the peelers and all. Even the hard men's worried. Word is you mention the subject to them they go buck mad. Like don't remind them. Hard enough to find out things as it is but this one's buried far as everybody's concerned. I don't know why you're so worried. There's enough going on every day to keep you busy for a month, even if you do find something out you've got an editor won't touch the stuff if it was money and I think he's right. Like nobody wants to read about it. Like nobody wants to see pictures of starving darkies on the TV. Somebody gets shot they don't mind so much. It's like the poor shot fucker could've got out of the road if he'd any sense and not stood in front of guns going off. Or maybe it's like he must of done something to deserve it. There's something official about getting shot with a gun. It's like the gas chamber, fucking guillotine. It's kind of legitimate. Like once you got a gun you got to have somebody to shoot at. Load the magazine, pull the trigger and whatever you're having yourself. But people don't want to read about maniacs cutting people up with knives.'

'You're wrong there. I know you're wrong. People love to read things like that. Innocent victim of sex fiend. Lapping it up. Sexual organs mutilated. Policemen with thirty years' experience controlling their emotions.'

'You're right. There's nothing like a set of mutilated sexual organs.'

'Or a partially undressed corpse. Signs of recent inter-course.'

'Like the slut must of done something to deserve it.'

'We're getting away from the point.'

'Are you looking for a conspiracy theory here.'

'Nothing like a good conspiracy theory when you're drinking in a bar, you don't know if you're going to get yourself shot for walking in the door just.'

'A cover-up at the highest level'd be better.'

'Fuck you.'

'Seriously.'

'Seriously fuck you.'

*

Ryan left Coppinger at the bar and emerged cautiously on to the Ormeau Road. To be seen coming out of the Gasworks could formally identify you as a target. You looked for cover. You watched the headlights of oncoming cars, staring into the filament. Engine notes were important. Military vehicles had a high-pitched diesel whine which made you think of curfew breaches, peremptory orders to halt, unexplained gunfire in the night. Even the sound of his own feet seemed illicit. He thought about the file of blurred photographs at the paper of those who disappeared without explanation. Photographs taken at birthday parties, family gatherings. A sense of the inevitable about the self-effacing smile. Something is being masked, the bitter knowledge that they will soon find themselves lost in the untenanted houses of the dead.

five

Dorcas said it was true she did conceal worries about Victor in her heart as anyone would. There was so much going on in the way of shootings and killings being committed on a regular basis and much of it covered up by government order as well. Though James once said not to worry, you had more chance of getting yourself hurt in a road crash or accident at work as you would have of getting shot – and he could prove it by statistics which surprised her. He could surprise you like that, she said, in the way he usually said nothing you thought he didn't know what was going on. She knew for instance he concealed a passionate nature once, though you wouldn't think it to look. It was a case of still waters.

But Victor had this gift to make you laugh. Even when he was young he could have you in stitches by mocking the neighbours or acting the big gangster he saw in the pictures. But there were times you would see an anger and a darkness there so that he would fight often with other children. He had as many sides to his nature you couldn't keep up. But he never raised his hand to her in all his born days nor would any son that loved his mother, though on occasions she put a strap to his backside taking no pleasure from it but being driven by a grim necessity of duty. When he was a child sometimes he would cry for no reason, which she understood as it was a frequent occurrence of her own nature, just starting for no reason when she was at the washing line or salt tears pricking her eyelids suddenly when she was out shopping so that at times she was driven to refuge in a public toilet in the city centre to stay there with the tears tripping her.

He had an eye for the women too. That was his father in him she thought. She had the opinion that women were an undue influence in his life. He was forever watching after them the way they walked and all. She reckoned that woman Heather had a hand in his destruction. To look at her you'd have thought that butter wouldn't melt. He said to Dorcas he could laugh with her which is what attracted him. She said to him she knew what attracted him: the big Zeppelins she had on her and the little girl voice. But she found him heedless of her concern although when he was visiting he left her outside in the car. She could see he was in a fog of lust with her around and said to him once did she come with a warning like a prescription from the chemist: do not drive or operate heavy machinery? It was a case of an old story at work from the start and he knew it not being able to look her in the eye.

After a job Victor would meet with the others in the Pot Luck to watch the evening news. It was an early ambition of his to have a job as first item on the news but then he became distrustful of the narrative devices employed. The newsreaders' neutral haircuts and accents, the careful placing of stresses to indicate condemnation or approval, the measured tones of reassurance. The suggestive, shifting vernacular used left Big Ivan more confused than anyone. He heard accounts of events he had been involved in which conflicted with his experience. He felt that rich portions of his memory were being snatched from him. Victor wondered if this had anything to do with Big Ivan's sudden conviction that he had been adopted at birth. He would read aloud stories of children abandoned in telephone boxes with scrawled notes describing their tiny marginal lives. One night he told Victor that he knew what his real parents were like. His father was tall and handsome. His mother had a resonant and ageless beauty, but both were concealers of a secret grief. Victor put on a face of concern when Big Ivan spoke of this, though in his private thoughts he considered that if he had been the father of a baby in the likeness of Big Ivan he would have abandoned if not strangled it.

When the unit's activities were mentioned on television Willie Lambe would give himself over to an uncritical delight. He imagined himself in later years being interviewed in front of the camera. His confident grasp of the issues raised. His early life. He would admit to dark times, lean periods when he struggled with despair but then explain the benefits of an optimistic nature and share insights gained through hardship. He would praise the role of family life.

That March Victor was asked to carry out a kneecap job on three members of the organization who had burgled an elderly woman's house. It was a question of discipline and maintaining the image of the organization. He knew that the men involved were members of the Gibraltar bar unit. Darkie Larche's men. It would be necessary to arrange a meeting in the Gibraltar to get clearance for the punishment. He didn't like this. He knew how Larche would react. The great Victor Kelly looking for permission. He could see Larche standing at the bar going this Kelly character doesn't know his arse from a hole in his trousers has to come to me and ask permission. Victor would walk into the Gibraltar and Larche would laugh and slap him on the back. Like he was some big friend. Hey, you behind the bar there, give my mate Victor a drink there, your fucking arm broke or something? The great Victor Kelly, come on with that drink there, your fucking leg tied to the piano?

When he had set up the meeting Victor planned the job down to the last detail. It was almost as if the punishments had been carried out. When he shut his eyes it was like watching a film with the volume turned down. He could see men bundled into a car, their faces obscured, brought to a secret location. The interrogation. The blue muzzle flash. He could see himself being driven away from the scene with the face of a man troubled in his heart. He thought that this must be what they called a premonition.

The meeting took place in the top room at the Gibraltar. Darkie Larche was there with three older men from the area. Victor sat down at the table. Darkie said nothing. The three older men looked like the frail members of a government in exile, deeply versed in the politics of failure. Victor put his case simply, projecting an air of humility. He listened while the three men gave the matter grave deliberation, reached agreement in principle. Darkie did not speak.

Downstairs Victor insisted on buying the drinks. A group of younger men gathered around him and he sensed that the three older men were uneasy in his presence. His sports jacket with checks that cost ninety pounds, his ability to cause bursts of nervous laughter, the deadly vacancy in his eyes. Occasionally Darkie looked across the room and raised his glass to him. Later in the night he called for silence in the bar. He said that he was pleased to see Victor there and welcomed the new spirit of co-operation. That Victor was welcome to join the Gibraltar unit at any time. He said that he himself did not personally believe rumours to the effect that Victor's father was a Catholic. The silence in the bar was maintained. Everyone was looking at each other with an awareness of hidden weapons. They knew that the insult could not go unanswered. The young men stepped back from Victor and the group around Darkie rearranged itself imperceptibly. Victor observed the way they all changed position, the choreographed movements leading towards a duel. He felt detached, interested in the outcome. This was an ability he had, to step outside himself, think on different levels. He had a sense of dusty main streets, the clink of spurs. Going to the pictures he had learned respect for the western showdown. Men working from necessities buried deep in their nature. The brief exchange of words as an acknowledgement of men puzzled beyond endurance. The heat. The formal desolation. Two men feeling marooned in the hinterland of their own desire. The smell of leather, gun oil and sweat.

Victor stepped away from the bar wondering how he could get to the Browning under his jacket. He could see the butt of a revolver in Darkie's belt. Then he felt the attention of the room shift to the door behind him. Risking a glance he saw Willie Lambe standing there with a police issue Walther in his hand. Suddenly everyone had guns, people were moving between him and Darkie. He considered taking out the Browning, blazing away. He could feel the three older men around him, talking gently, moving him towards the door.

'Car's waiting, Victor.'

Heather saw Victor for the first time at one of the parties. He came in with two others. The first thing she noticed was his black curly hair and dark skin so at first she thought that he was foreign, a sailor off one of the boats. She had a weakness for men with foreign looks. He looked like he might think in another language. She wondered if he might be an Arab. She had read somewhere that Arabs liked plump women and she imagined him discussing the plumpness of women in a strange and cruelly shaped alphabet. He looked like a man who carried within a tense coil of stored words capable of describing rare and dangerous sexual acts. The congress of the snake.

When Darkie came in she asked him who he was. Darkie barely looked towards him.

'Dangerous territory. That's the famous Victor Kelly. Flash bastard. Thinks he's God's gift to women, sun, moon and stars shine out of his fly.'

'I thought he was a foreigner,' she said, giggling.

'Could say that, supposed to be his da's a Taig from the Falls.'

'They say Taigs is good at it.'

'Don't.'

'What?'

'Just fucking don't.'

'What are you looking at me like that for?'

Darkie had a sensation of faint recollection as if he was twenty years from that moment and stirred by a particular memory.

'What look?'

'That kind of sad parting look. That fond farewell look. Kind of all the good times we had together sort of a look.'

'I haven't a baldy what you're on about.'

Since the parties had started she had seen less of Darkie during the week. When they met he was reluctant to touch her as though the time they had spent together was inscribed on her skin, faint outlines easily erased. He subjected her to long silences so that she had become an authority on the types of male silence. There were silences of sorrowful reproof. Fond silences. Dumb silences. Doubtful silences. Nursing of wounds silences. There were the profound viral silences belonging to the terminally ill.

'Introduce me.'

'What?'

'I have to say everything twice to you these days. Introduce me. I want to meet him.'

Heather knew he would refuse. Later she approached the group by the window. They were talking and laughing among themselves in the alcove formed by the velvet curtains she had bought herself in Corry's. Darkie said she was picking whore-house furnishings but she didn't care. She loved the touch of the red fabric and the way it made you want to rub against it.

The three men stopped talking and looked up as she came towards them. It was like an oriental scene from a film she had watched. Suddenly she felt as if she could go down on her knees, make ritual gestures of submission and repentance. The other two were impassive, unimpressed by the way she found herself walking, swaying from the hips, eyes downcast. Victor moved sideways on the sofa to make room for her. She sat down.

Later she said he had these blue eyes could see right through you. After a while she noticed that Big Ivan and Willie Lambe were drunk out of the mind. It was like the way they were most of the time, locked, so that they hardly knew what they were doing. Not Victor. He was Mr X-Ray with this good smell off his leather jacket and aftershave, a bottle of which he kept in the glove compartment of his car, a new one every week. His personal habits were very good also. He gave her a cigarette and took one and lit them both with a gold Dunhill lighter. But he was hardly what you would call a smoker, she said; he would spend his time looking along the butt like it was a gun barrel or blowing smoke rings to make you laugh like some-body's uncle, but it was really like a cigarette was something he found dropped from the sky he didn't know what to do with.

She said that it wasn't hard to guess from the way she talked that she was smitten straight off which was the God's honest truth not something she ever wished to hide. She was mad for him like no other man. He could make her cream herself just by looking. She said she could have had him there on the sofa or anything and you could tell he felt that way too. Without a word being spoken they went to the spare bedroom which she kept locked at parties because of a horror of walking in on a couple which would make her feel used in her own body. Before they got in bed he took out this big gun he had stuck in his belt and spun it around in his hand all the time watching himself in the mirror on the wardrobe with an expression of being somewhere else completely, until she said to him come here, please, hurry up. I can't bear it.

*

44

Afterwards they went for a drive in his car. Victor always had energy, a terror of sitting still. Sometimes Heather saw him act like an escaped prisoner with involuntary backward glances as if there were dogs on his tail. They moved carefully among the sleeping bodies on the living-room floor. Victor made a game of it, pretending to stumble and put his foot in someone's mouth, bringing it down an inch to the side of the person's head. He did this in slow motion so Heather could hardly bear it, choking back giggles. She had a feeling that McClure was awake and watching them. Nothing she could put her finger on. Just somebody's eyes open, a glimpse of intrigue in the dark.

Dawn had broken. There was a fine drizzle falling and Heather laughed at the way rain beaded in Victor's hair like a hairnet you'd see an old woman wearing. He took a firing position outside the house and pretended to shoot down a seagull. His hand described it falling, arcing across the city. He made the sound of a crippled engine with his lips, the sound of a fuselage crumping on impact, exploding in a blaze of aviation fuel. Games. They drove slowly about the city. At first Heather thought he was driving at random; then she saw the pattern. He was driving carefully along the edges of Catholic west Belfast. She had never been this close before although she had seen these places on television. Ballymurphy, Andersonstown. The Falls. Names resonant with exclusion. Now they were circling the boundaries, close enough to set foot in them. Victor drove up into the foothills until they were looking down on the west of the city, its densely populated and mythic new estates, something you didn't quite believe in. He looked down at it then turned to her. You never ask what where I've been or what I've been doing, he said. Never. You don't even think, he said. Yes, Victor, she said. He stopped the engine and reached for her. She thought he wanted to do it within sight of the enemy. He pointed out different parts of the city to her. New Lodge. The Short Strand.

He described how you could wipe them off the map from here. Artillery fire directed with precision. Repeated sorties. She could feel his excitement at the idea. He saw himself as a general conducting pre-dawn briefings with a roomful of men with drawn faces, targets circled on a map. He pulled her towards him and undid the buttons on her blouse then slipped his hand inside her bra without unfastening it so that he could feel the floral pattern at the top pressing into his hand. They stayed like that, her head turned towards him with a kind of disbelief in her eyes. The nylon left a mark on the back of his hand which did not fade until that afternoon. A ceremonial motif, relic of some half-forgotten rite.

Later that day Willie Lambe and Big Ivan picked up Jimmy Craig, Ian Morris and Frames McCrea for the burglary. They brought them to the back room of the Pot Luck where they waited for Victor. The atmosphere was relaxed. Big Ivan went to the bar to get twenty Embassy Regal for Ivor Morris. The Pot Luck team were courteous, enquiring after wives and girl-friends. They apologized for the drab surroundings and the delay in Victor's arrival. They spoke among themselves in hushed, sympathetic tones. Willie Lambe kept looking nervously at his watch and Jimmy Craig reassured him. Take her easy there, Willie. We know Victor's kept busy, man can't be in two places at once. Frames McCrea was the only one who said nothing. After Frames had got out on bail he had started to look old. His forehead was deeply lined. He suffered from waking suddenly at night, intimations of mortality. It seemed as if he had discovered an exhausting and terminal truth while he was in full flight through the city centre in a stolen car. One hundred and sixty-four checkpoints. People pointed him out in the street. The site where he had launched the car over a checkpoint on to the motorway ramp was visited by children, and he had not developed the means to fend off their awe, the grim reticence of the exalted and solitary.

The mood changed when Victor came in. He wanted a flawless exercise he said. He was talking in terms of operational details. He had arranged for three separate cars to be waiting outside and that someone be waiting at the lock-up garage where the kneecappings were to take place. He talked about integral planning. He had adopted an officer's stance, legs apart, his hands behind his back holding the Browning loosely. He talked about the robbery. An innocent old woman robbed in her home then tied up and left alone until a neighbour released her. The joint pains. The thoughts of her grandchildren, their bright and eternal faces under blond hair and her uncertain efforts to retain their names. He talked about the evening sun shining in through her bedroom window on to the faded wallpaper. His voice was kindly and reproachful. Craig and McCrea hung their heads but Ian Morris looked him straight in the face.

'We never done it, Victor,' he said, 'we never done a thing like that.'

Victor nodded to Big Ivan who hit Morris with his fist on the side of the head. Willie Lambe hit Craig. Big Ivan kicked McCrea. Victor continued. The three men had spent the day in the Gibraltar buying drinks from the proceeds of the robbery. The barman had described the notes smelling of mothballs. The money the old woman had kept to pay her funeral expenses, a bitter-scented currency of dissolution. Willie Lambe hit Craig backhanded. Big Ivan kicked Morris in the kidneys and headbutted McCrea.

'Me and you's mates, Victor,' Morris said. 'You know me. I wouldn't go and rob one of our own for fuck's sake.'

'Fucking graverobbers,' Big Ivan said, knocking him over.

'Old lady could of died, fucking circulation suffocated the fuck out of her tied up like that,' Willie Lambe said, thinking about his own mother, the way her feet got cold at night.

Victor knew that it could go on like that all day. He stepped forward and put the barrel of the Browning against each man's forehead in turn and told them they had thirty seconds to tell the truth and shame the devil. The gun barrel left a mark between each man's eyes and their faces were tense and fixed so that they looked like the members of a sect devoted to moments of urgent revelation. In the end it was Frames McCrea who gave them the details. It was a spare account. They had ignored the fact that they would almost definitely be caught. This blindness, he seemed to be saying, had led him to question his motives. Craig entered a plea for clemency. Morris turned to Willie, pointed at his temple with a forefinger and raised his eyebrows. Willie shook his head, smiling.

'No problem Ian. No nut jobs today. We're just drilling kneecaps.'

The three men were escorted outside and into the cars. Big Ivan, Hacksaw McGrath and Victor were to be the firing party. Willie Lambe had to leave to bring his mother to the shops. Big Ivan was annoyed at the inclusion of Hacksaw. Hacksaw was a mad dog, Big Ivan said. Victor explained that Hacksaw needed to be blooded as part of a precision operation.

On the way to the garage Victor talked to Ian Morris about greyhounds. Morris was an acknowledged expert and had formulated a plan for introducing Arab racing dogs to the city's tracks. He kept two of them in his backyard. Salukis. So far they had refused to let him get within five yards of them. He had been brooding on this, watching them from the kitchen window, the fine-boned disdainful way they had of walking, their lack of proper import documentation. He imagined them running at Dunmore Park, describing the anatomy of a desert wind in heart-stopping record circuits. Victor was sympathetic.

Inside the garage there were three clean revolvers sitting neatly on a workbench. A rotating Castrol sign moved gently on its axis when they entered. McCrea seemed relieved to enter the familiar gloom, strewn with car-parts, a place devoted to the principles of dismantling. Victor told them to lie face-down on the floor. Craig said that he didn't want to ruin the new suit he had bought the week before. Big Ivan pointed out that he was going to shoot him through the trousers anyway. This hadn't occurred to Craig. He lay down, grimacing as he lowered his body on to the floor. Victor told the Pot Luck men to stand over each one and wait for his signal. They were to fire a single shot into the back of each knee. He paused for a moment to permit a gathering of thoughts.

Afterwards he would wonder in private what was going through Frames McCrea's head. Whether he had seized on some imaginary reserve of immunity left over after Constable McMinn had knocked him sideways off Amelia Street into the side of a parked lorry where he had stayed with his head resting on the wheel and the speedometer jammed at eighty-three until firemen arrived to cut the clutch pedal from around his foot. Perhaps the circumstances had awakened the impulse to flight that had led him towards stealing cars in the first place. Victor saw him get to his feet and look around slowly. Victor was surprised to see a faintly aggrieved look that he had seen on his own mother's face often. It expressed resentment at the encroachment of life and of the memories she had made for herself, their slow accumulation and drag. He began to run towards the garage door. To Big Ivan it seemed as if he had discovered another gravitational field within the confines of the garage. His legs seemed to be moving with the same buoyant steps that men with bulky suits had made on the moon. Out of the corner of his eye Victor saw Hacksaw raise his revolver and aim with the preoccupied and stately air of a child sighting on an imaginary Indian. He shot McCrea once in the back so that he fell forward on to his face and lay without moving. Victor went over to inspect him then told the others to resume their positions, reflecting that you only ever achieve an approximation of what you desire.

six

Artie Wilson was transferred from Crumlin Road to the Downshire Hospital with a psychiatric report stating that he was suffering from paranoid delusions. He thought that someone was going to kill him. Staff at the Downshire tried to reassure him. They explained to him that the hospital doors were locked against killers that might stalk his nights. Allegorical figures with shuffling walks and pale speculative eyes. They understood his fears. There is something about an institutional corridor which lends itself to raw fear. The shining tiles. The antiseptic distances.

Wilson, who was from the Village, had been convicted of selling cartridges for an unlicensed shotgun to a Catholic and given two years. The two men had shared receding memories of duckhunting at dusk on Lough Neagh. Crouched in a punt offshore waiting for the clipped arctic beat of wings coming towards them out of the darkest part of the October sky, until it seemed a kind of grace to be there as witness to vast and incurious migrations from the North. They knew there had to be consequences. Wilson had asked to be held in solitary confinement in Crumlin Road prison to protect him from the loyalist prisoners. It gave him time to think about the nature of betrayal. He borrowed books about the great traitors from the prison library. Lundy, Casement. It seemed to him that his own error in consorting with a Catholic was minor compared to these men whose deceits were concerned with the future of nations.

At the Downshire they counted the knives after dinner and

locked up toxic paints after art therapy class which led him to think about suicide. On television he watched pictures of girls who had been tarred and feathered for going out with British soldiers. They were left dangling from lampposts like crude fetishes designed to ward off a vengeance of intimate proportions. He remembered having seen it happen in the Village to a girl who was engaged to a Catholic. The women had shaved the girl's head indoors while the men stood around outside with the tar and feathers, smoking and chatting. It seemed a form of initiation prescribed by custom.

When he was returned to Crumlin Road he would lie awake at night in the pilgrim darkness waiting for the metal shutter of the judas hole to slide back.

At the beginning of September he was released on two weeks' parole. At home he was quiet and reflective, attentive to his family and to his parole officer. He was surprised at how difficult it was to find his way back to his old life. It seemed to be a thing requiring skills of navigation accompanied by prayers and invocations and he was ignorant of them. On his last night he opened the front door to a smiling man in a black leather jacket who said he wanted to buy a shotgun.

'You must have the wrong house.'

'I don't think so. It's not a bad evening. Good for shooting.'

'I suppose.'

'Ducks.'

'Too much glare. They'd come in at you out of the sun before you knew where you were,' Artie Wilson said, knowing he was lost.

'Or Taigs.' There was a black Capri on the other side of the road with another man leaning on the bonnet looking at him with the kind of passionate disinterest people reserve for victims of serious car accidents lying on roadside verges. Victor took a revolver out of its pocket and pressed it to Wilson's side just below his heart.

'Or traitors,' he suggested in a whisper.

*

In Castlereagh Interrogation Centre Victor was fingerprinted then photographed front and profile. Looking good, Victor. He knew that these photographs were important, that in the future they could be released to the press. When he took a comb out of his pocket and smoothed his hair back none of the policemen objected. There was a silent acceptance of his sense of privilege. He was escorted from room to room gently. He began to suspect that they had a good case against him.

He was brought to an interview room. He recognized the detective who entered.

'How's about you, Herbie. Haven't seen you this good while. Thought you was transferred.'

'I seen you though, Victor. I was keeping a wee eye out for you.'

Victor laughed out loud to show he was aware of the direction things were taking. That he knew how policemen were attracted to the ominous statement.

'You're a hard nut, Victor, isn't that right?'

'See my new motor when you were watching me, Herbie? The Capri?'

'I suppose you're going to tell me where you got the money to buy it?'

'That's right, Herbie, I'm going to break down and confess.'

'I know you are Victor. You're going to cry like a baby and tell us you wish you never done it, you just don't know what come over you.'

'Capri's a flying machine, Herbie. Give us a shout someday, I'll give you a run in her.'

Each man chose his words carefully. They knew that ordinary speech was inadequate to the occasion. The exchange was carefully staged. At the start they were using the tones of flawed irony employed in gangster films, weary and laced with knowledge of the relentless nature of human greed and cruelty. Later they would move towards the process of questioning, a language of lovers prone to nuance and revelation, sensitive to pain.

'You're a good-looking boy, Victor, a real charmer.'

'You know how it is, Herbie.'

'We got some eye-witnesses in a line-up downstairs to admire you, Victor. Women and all. Just dying to get a look at the great Victor Kelly. Seen you do Artie Wilson, so they did. I'm sure you won't object.'

'You know me, Herbie, always willing and eager to help the law.'

'This won't take a second, Victor.'

Victor joined four other men in the identification parade. The others all wore leather jackets, cheaper than the one Victor had. The brightness of the room highlighted the lines on their faces. They exuded an air of disappointment, unfulfilled lives. Somewhere it seemed they had been found wanting and brought, haggard and unshaven, to this windowless room, a place of unwavering judgement. There was a stir when the eye-witnesses were brought in. They waited in the darkness behind the bright lights. Victor could sense their attentiveness, the way they held their breath in the face of the choice they were about to make.

'Face front.'

Victor turned into the lights and gave them a dangerous smile which he had practised in front of the mirror. It was a Cagney smile, elegant and derisive. It showed that he had invulnerability to spare. Then he began to walk towards the lights. At first no one reacted. The other men in the line-up exchanged glances. He stepped in front of the lights and peered into the darkness with one hand shading his eyes. He looked bewildered now, deprived of familiar landmarks. Two uniformed policemen grabbed him from behind.

'I'm fucking innocent,' he shouted. 'I never done nothing. I'm a victim of brutality. I been wrong accused of this crime. I got mental conditions the police took advantage of.'

Hand-cuffed to two policemen Victor waited outside the line-up room. The detective came out.

'Good try, Victor.'

'You like that, Herbie?'

'Very good. You should of been in fucking films.'

'Sorry about the identification evidence, Herbie. As you say, I don't know what come over me. And here's you with all this evidence you can't use no more since my brief's going to get up on the hind legs in court and say your honour this here evidence is flawed because my client went and made a show of himself in front of the witnesses and that's why they're identifying him and after all the trouble you took.'

'Is that a fact Victor?'

'Afraid so. You see I always took this keen amateur interest in the law and it says all the people in a line-up's got to behave the same way. Still and all, it's good to see you take it generous.'

'The thing is Victor you're going to have to stay with us for a while till I get this sorted out and see if we can't come up with an accomplice and figure out a way to let him know that this running round the place, shooting everybody in sight, is not a very mature activity and maybe he'll tell us a story and maybe you being a famous person's going to be in this story.'

'That's very fucking comical, Herbie, you practise that or something?'

'Natural talent is all, Victor, natural talent.'

It was a shock to Dorcas when she heard that Victor was in the prison for murder. Although she knew that in times of rioting and disorder in the streets the police and courts were subject to errors in their thinking it never entered her mind that Victor would fall victim. It was exactly the ordeal a mother dreads. She was in a crippled apprehension for news in the first week but no information was forthcoming to her. Day after day she went to police stations to sit in grim thoughts while the police took not a blind bit of notice of her. The idea that she once placed faith in the police was a source of bitter laughter.

It was a normal thing in such circumstances to blame God

and be in dismay. But this was a temptation to which she resisted with all her might. Instead she took Big Ivan's suggestion that it was a case of mistaken identity. Though when Big Ivan said it first she felt at that moment that Victor was not himself but somebody else unknown. Or like identity withheld until next of kin are informed. She thought that it was a strange thing in families to become suddenly unknown to each other through thought or deed.

During those four weeks before he was released she had to go each Thursday on a minibus to visit, along with other women who had family in Crumlin Road. She did not wish to pass unnecessary judgement, but simply to say that some of them lacked anything which could be described as manners. She would pass over many of the things that came out of their mouths as words were not adequate. She was often fit for nothing by the time the minibus passed through the prison gate.

Being searched was a further tribulation, being sometimes required to remove garments, which was a large matter and not helped by the commonplace remarks of other women.

She regarded it as a sad matter for a mature woman to be in a place where men were caged like the beasts of the field. It recalled to her the cattle pens at the docks that were a part of her childhood, the pens being full of the sound of metal gates to wake the dead and a smell that rancoured in your nostrils as well. She thought at the time that all those animals bound for slaughter was an offence to innocence.

In addition it was not permitted by regulation to bring Victor a few small things of comfort, such as Tayto crisps or soda bread. There was also an atmosphere of damp to compare to their first house where clothes left in a wardrobe went mouldy overnight. It was an ease to her worry, though, that Victor was a Trustee prisoner from the start. Trust our Victor, she would say, and shake her head so that it could be seen that she was rueful but also proud.

When she went into the visiting room he was usually sat

there before her with that grin on that made you want to slap and also hug him. Of course she could not lay a hand across the table in light of warning notices that attempts to make physical contact will result in immediate termination of visit. At first it seemed that the desk where they sat was a great gulf separating mother and son. He was dark-skinned by nature but underneath he was pale. James told her once that sunlight was necessary to put vitamins in the skin. One of the foolish things he would say with the intention no doubt of putting the fear of God into her heart. A man who would go to football matches but would not come to visit his son. She knew there was nothing in it. But still a mother's natural woe.

Well son, she would always begin, and then they would sit there with nothing to say like persons who are facing a great jeopardy. She would feel as if her tongue and lips had betrayed her or that somehow words had been denied. She felt these encounters onerous. It was not something she could easily bear except that Victor seemed to have a light of understanding of this problem in his eye. At such times it seemed as if the whole room had stopped in a description of eternity. It occurred to her that speech itself is a cruel deceiver or kind of hoax which could not be relied upon. This fact was an ache felt in her breast. It left a taste as if of ashes in her mouth. When it seemed they had reached a pitch of silence to overtake endurance, a type of humming in the ears, Victor would find words like a man describing with hesitance a turning point in his life or a time he thought he would die but didn't. He told her the routine of his day, which did not vary. The quietness of his nights without a soul. She saw then that he would not go to seed or fall into brooding. Someone, he said, had told him how great men had found thoughts to guide them for the rest of their lives during dreary prison nights. The result was she felt assurance and when people on the street stopped to ask her, how's Victor? she was able to answer them with cheerfulness. Although she had misgivings from the start that the world would seek to thwart his high objective. It brought a nightly tear to her eye to think of him there in a dark cell turning things over in his head and perhaps going to the window to stare through the bars. She wondered if she had found the words to advise him would he have taken her advice so that she was not now heartrended.

seven

Ryan noticed how newspapers and television were developing a familiar and comforting vocabulary to deal with violence. Sentences which could be read easily off the page. It involved repetition of key phrases. Atrocity reports began to achieve the pure level of a chant. It was no longer about conveying information. It was about focusing the mind inwards, attending to the durable rhythms of violence.

Coppinger pointed out how the essential details of an attack, the things which differentiated one incident from another, were missing. Points which he considered vital were being omitted from eyewitness accounts. Whether the killer spoke the victim's name before firing. Whether or not the victim wore a mask, a combat jacket, a boilersuit. It was rare for paramilitaries to wear a stocking mask. It was a question of vanity. It made you look like an ancient bare-knuckle boxer. It suggested mild brain damage. Parkas were popular, berets, sunglasses. The black balaclava was a favourite and Coppinger held that this was due to commando films popular in the city. The Cockleshell Heroes.

They agreed that the reporting of violent incident was beginning to diverge from events. News editors had started to re-work their priorities, and government and intelligence agencies were at work. Paramilitaries escorted journalists to secret locations where they posed with general purpose machineguns and RPG7 rocket launchers. Car bombings were carried out to synchronize with news deadlines.

Coppinger was following up incidents where the attackers went unmasked.

'It means they're cocky bastards. It means they don't give a shit if they get caught. Else it means they're protected somehow.'

Ryan gave it a more ominous meaning. The killer was compelled to form a liaison with the victim. To wear their fear and disbelief like a garment of compulsive desire. It was the full-screen close-up: the lips parted, the eyes half-closed, the rapt expression.

It was eleven o'clock on Saturday morning when Coppinger rang Ryan at his flat on the junction of the Antrim Road and the Cavehill Road. Ryan had been drinking in the Markets the night before. He had started to take on the role of the lone drinker. He went to bars where he would not be recognized, drinking heavily. He began to regard it as an austere calling, demanding stamina and focus. After a while he started to recognize others. Slight men around fifty years old with flecked lips and watery red eyes as if from endless contemplation of limited resources. Starting in the afternoon they moved from bar to bar, having no more than one or two drinks in each. Normally they sat beside a doorway, sometimes moving their lips as if to address some verified and private rancour. He had paid them little attention before although he had seen them sitting in a packed bar at closing time or walking home with their heads down. Contained, resentful, unhurried. It was the most dangerous time of night. There was no activity on the street and the men followed the same route each time. It seemed like an invitation to violence, abduction, drive-past shootings, but they were oblivious to the threat. They were sunk in delusion and indifference and other devices of the solitary.

Ryan began to walk home alone himself. Often taxis would not come to the bars he frequented. Normally he would pass through the city centre to the bottom of the Antrim Road. The city centre had been heavily bombed with the emphasis on

commercial premises. These attacks had glamour. Damage estimates running into six figures were quoted with admiration, part of an awesome and impersonal civic expenditure.

Once he had gone from Royal Avenue to the Antrim Road the dereliction was on a more intimate scale. Acres of pre-war housing had been abandoned because of intimidation. The windows and doorways had been bricked up. The official explanation for this was to prevent vandalism and arson, but Ryan always felt an overwhelming sense of violently interrupted lives when he walked past. He imagined the houses kept spotlessly clean, the doorsteps worn from scrubbing. It was a dark place. These streets retained a sense of worked lives. It was for this that the windows and doors were bricked, to restrain vengeful domestic spirits.

Often he passed small groups of youths, a metallic taste of alcohol in his mouth. His walk was a drunk's precarious experiment with motion, a struggle with memory. He felt it offered immunity. It drew on an ancient respect for the afflicted and infirm. The youths wore Wrangler jackets and parallel jeans. He could not anticipate their reactions. You had to know the structure of the gang. The implacable codes.

When the telephone rang he was looking at himself in the bathroom mirror. Attempting to distinguish age and damage from the glass's liverspots and seeping watermarks. He wondered how long it would take before he began to resemble the men who drifted from pub to pub. The bleakness. The dark thought that no longer beholds itself.

'O'Neill's Car Parts warehouse,' Coppinger said. He pronounced each word carefully and Ryan knew that he had been drinking. He thought of a pilot losing altitude, a last positional report.

'The location is right for our boys. Between the Falls and the Shankill. Easy access. Four men without masks. There are four dead, two men shot in the back of the head while in a kneeling position.'

'Robbery?'

'There's no money missing as far as anyone can tell. Apparently all they took was two headlights for a fucking Ford Capri.'

'What makes you think it's the same people did the knife jobs?'

'I'm telling you, you go sniffing about this place looking for who done this one there'll be a massive big silence. Like nobody talking. People looking over their shoulders. People making excuses not to meet you. There's something about it.'

'What?'

'The two men made to kneel.'

'What? Prayer? Attitude of submission.'

'Something there yes, and no money took or anything. Except the headlights. Too impatient to rob the place. Fucking bodies all over the place and somebody thinking there's a new headlight for the car, I'll have that. There's blood everyplace. There's a smell of cordite and this fucker's taking headlights.'

'Petty.'

'Yes.'

'Doesn't give a shit.'

'No. Something else.'

'Gratuitous.'

'That's not it. It's the calculation in it. The insult to the dead.'

'Maybe.'

There was a wistful pause in which they were both aware of the telephone line between them, miles of resonant cable. The speech of the city. A dreamtime of voices. A residual hum on the line like the vexed, insistent voices of the dead. Ryan was still holding the receiver in his hand minutes after Coppinger had hung up, dried shaving foam on his face. He wiped it off with a towel and ran the hot tap again. Please. Kill me.

Victor and his team were in the Pot Luck celebrating the O'Neill job. Following the collapse of the identification evidence the

police had no grounds to hold him and he had felt that a big job was needed to mark his return. Big Ivan was behind the bar setting up the large bottles of Red Hand as fast as he could move. Victor was playing darts with Willie Lambe. The bar was listening open-mouthed to Big Ivan's history of obscenity. It was late afternoon and they had been there since eleven o'clock, sunshine coming in through the window. A day you couldn't put the brakes on.

'You and me, Victor,' Willie Lambe was saying, putting his arm around Victor's shoulders. 'You and me, the best of mates, right?' He moved closer to Victor's ear. Victor laughed and pushed him away. Physical contact between men was a thing he disliked.

Willie had a scheme. He knew where they could rob a tanker of alcohol from an industrial alcohol plant. They would syphon it into 40-ounce Blue Smirnoff bottles and sell it to Taig pubs who'd take anything they could lay their greedy mitts on, he knew that for a fact. The raw alcohol would cause blindness, impotence and other unknown symptoms exclusive to the destitute of heart.

'Armaggedon,' Willie whooped, 'the wrath of Victor.'

Victor recognized it as a bootleg plan which belonged on celluloid. Heavily laden trucks going without headlights on a precarious road skirting the edges of uncertainty. He had other things on his mind. The quiet face on Hacksaw McGrath after they had done the two in the office. The fact that McGrath hadn't been seen since. He had already got Big Ivan to ditch the weapons.

Heather watched them from the bar. When she liked she could withdraw into her mind so it was as if she wasn't there. She thought of herself as disconnected at these moments. The men treated her with absentminded gentleness. She was the only woman permitted to sit in at these gatherings. She would withdraw into the stance of a domestic mascot whose presence bestowed indulgence without obligation.

When Victor was around Big Ivan treated Heather as an

accomplice in matters of love and consulted her on the doings of women. It was a perpetual problem for him. He put his longing on furtive display for her like some valuable treasure removed by looters, a fragile reliquary with associations of national yearning. Big Ivan acted as if it had fallen unwanted into his hands. He wanted to make amends for possessing it.

Willie Lambe kept a photograph of his mother on the dashboard of his car. His mother was twenty years old in the photograph, pretty, with a skin that suggested lacquer. Willie showed Victor the photograph. She looks like a film star from a silent picture, Victor said. Louise Brooks. Some malnourished heroine fading out of earshot. Victor laughed when Heather asked him about the mother. Fucking acts like she's a film star too, he said. He had been in the house which Willie shared with his mother. She was surrounded by photographs of herself in her youth. The photographs were arranged in groups on small tables. There were themes of gaiety, companionship, eternal youth. She smoked white-tipped menthol cigarettes, and the butts coated in lipstick smouldered in gift ashtrays. She was a fucking dried-up old hag who treated Willie like a slave, Victor said. Willie wags the tail when she pats the head, he said. Themes of cruelty, maternal neglect.

Heather noticed that each time Victor established a pattern he would break it. He would stay two or three nights at her flat then disappear for days. He never travelled by the same route. He never fucked her the same way twice in a row. He arrived with unexpected gifts. He would awake from varied nightmares. A gift for survival, he called it, secrets of a fugitive heart. One night he told her how John Dillinger had undergone plastic surgery to avoid detection. Victor was deeply impressed by the possibilities of transformation. To see yourself altered beyond recognition in a mirror. Heather said imagine looking in the mirror and seeing a squint and a double chin. Imagine seeing Big Ivan. I like you the way you are, she said.

Victor told her to continue with the parties in the flat. He explained to her that McClure was compiling dossiers. He showed her photographs that McClure had given him. She realized that many of them had been taken in her own flat. There were naked bodies on floors and in beds. They seemed unsurprised by the flashlight, as if the sight of each other's bodies had already confirmed sorrowful predictions. There were tapes as well, which he played on the car stereo. These were full of noises of sad recognition, a bleak interior language in which it seemed that irretrievable losses were being mourned.

McClure had policemen, civil servants and intelligence personnel in his portfolio. It was a case of finding a vice and exploiting it. He explained to Victor that he was concerned with extending the limits of human tolerance, pushing the victims of blackmail to the edge of logic. There had been suicides, which he regarded as defeat.

McClure had introduced Victor to amphetamine. Using a knife he had cut the top off a Benzidrex nasal inhaler and removed the cotton insert which he tore in half. He gave one piece to Victor, showing him how to dip it in milk to deaden its bitter chemical taste with overtones of dumped chemicals, slow leakage and genetic damage.

They spent the afternoon in a house on Crimea Street. Victor remembered sun in the room elaborated through the nylon net curtains on the small window, a sustaining lightfall. It seemed that they employed the speech of a seemly diplomacy — fluent protocols exchanged across a table by soft-spoken men whose words were accompanied by elegant gestures of goodwill. McClure made strong black coffee to boost the amphetamine. Their words had a soft gleam of meaning. Victor explained the discrimination he had suffered from, being mistaken for a Catholic because of the name Kelly. Their detestation of Catholics was a companionable thing. They agreed upon it as a resource requiring careful nurture.

McClure explained his attraction to the Nazis. Their elimination of remorse. The doctrinal simplicity. The massed voices and hushed stadiums. The defined oratorical sorrows.

He opened a cupboard and showed Victor a book which had been produced in Berlin in 1940. The German title was printed in heavy Gothic type, sharp-edged alien characters which seemed beyond anything that could be shaped by the palate. Each page had a single photographic plate of a nude boy who stared at the camera with a sombre, violated gaze.

'People's looking for control,' McClure said. 'They want somebody to take over, decide things for them, what to do with their lives. They'll hand over their life and cry tears of fucking gratitude that somebody else'll take it on for them. All that misery and deciding. They want to dress up and act the hero and fuck the rest. They'll die for that.'

Victor heard music approaching down the road. They went to the front door. Orangemen were returning from the dedication of a new banner, accompanied by several flute bands. The Orangemen walked in ranks between the bands wearing orange silk collarettes and black bowler hats. Two of them carried the banner showing William of Orange on a white charger. Their faces seemed distorted to Victor, as if they had witnessed some corrosive spectacle. The sunlight struck the metal fittings of the drums and flutes and the flute-players dipped their instruments to the rhythm of the march.

eight

Statement of John Arthur McGrath:

I John McGrath would like to state that the events I describe in the following happened as if in a dream so that it was as if I did not participate although I know that I did and this is a source of regret to me. We drove up to the gate of O'Neill's depot at ten o'clock in the morning of 10 May 1975. I remember a sign Trade Only at the gate which gave me a moment of panic at being recognized as not being trade. I felt foreign to my own nature from that moment. We stopped the car at the entrance to the warehouse. We got out and walked in. Mr C's eyes were lit up and he looked from side to side as if his head was afflicted by madness which I also started to feel, although I had no notion of a bloodbath at this or any other point. I do not wish to give the full name of Mr C.

There was another man with us who I also do not wish to name as he is notorious for being involved in killing and has not a spark of mercy in his nature. This man I shall call Mr M. He had wrote out this car parts order which was a fake on a piece of paper tore from a children's exercise book. He seemed to be in high good spirits at this point. Two assistants came up to us and Mr M handed one the note but before they could read it Mr C had them covered with a gun he took from his pocket and he said lie down on the ground. They lay down at that point.

Then Mr M said where's the office? One of the assistants looked up at us and pointed. I would like to say that there was no look of fear on his face or on the other one's. They seemed to lie down in a kind of blind disbelief. I remember Mr C said we should've brought a van and took some of the car parts that were sitting round the place but M said we were there for the money. M kept looking at me and saying things like are you all right and smiling at me to make me feel part of things. Apart from the incident with Frames which was a mistake with a gun going off by accident this was the first time I ever done anything like that and I hope I will never be involved again. This is a statement of my remorse.

M indicated that I should go with him to the office. I cannot remember how he said it or if he used words at all. We went up these old wooden steps which creaked with a noise to wake the dead. M seemed to change somehow as we went up as if it was a climb to murder. He had these blue eyes which seemed to get smaller and he did not speak.

The office had two glass windows looking over the depot and a glass door. There were two men inside. They looked up and seen me and M outside the glass. You could see them looking nervous and talking to each other but you couldn't hear them through the glass. Seeing them and all it was still like they weren't really there. It was like watching an event that happened some time ago recorded. M opened the door and we went in.

I had never been in a proper office before and it was just like you imagined a real one, or one on television. There were green filing cabinets and a desk with this big typewriter on it. I had this notion to type my name on it like a typist with big fingernails but M saw me and said not to do it.

The older man came forward and asked what we wanted. He had grey hair and was like your uncle or someone you know well who gives you that look like he was disappointed in you but not surprised to tell the truth. M said that we come for the money and that we were serious. He said it was early on Monday morning and that there was no money yet in a voice like everybody knows that. The younger one didn't say nothing but just looked at us. I am sorry for the younger one. M said for them both to kneel on the floor. The older man looked at him and he said it again to kneel.

I am of the belief now that robbery was not the motive for the actions of M on that day and that he had the whole thing planned from the start. There have been questions as to the mental state of M in that period and I would like to state that there was no sign of madness from when we reached the office but that he was calm and smiling during the incidents described.

When they were kneeling on the floor with their backs to us M put his gun to the older man's neck and I put my gun to the younger man's neck who started to say something. I think it was a Roman Catholic prayer. This seemed to cause displeasure to M. He fired his gun and mine went off also. I remember nothing of the office after that except that there was more smoke from the guns than you would think and that it gave you a taste in your mouth like when you touch a battery with your tongue to see if there is still any power left in it.

We went out of the office. Downstairs we saw that the other two were shot as well. M went behind the counter and looked until he saw headlights for his car. There was much laughter and talk in the car on the way back and no mention of the money. M said that I done well but I knew what would happen if I opened my mouth. I wish to say that I have now embraced Christian values and express repugnance at my deeds and that having made this clean breast I am at ease now in Christ.

nine

Persistent bombing began to alter the outlines of the town centre. The tallest buildings were demolished, so that it seemed as though some inscrutable intent was at work; looking towards the bay from the slopes of the Cavehill you began to detect the alien skyline of some ancient plundered city. People were displaying new forms of anxiety, and the membership of evangelical churches was increasing rapidly. There was a rise in the number of informers shot. They were abducted from their houses at night and found hooded and gagged in alleyways or on roadside verges outside the city. During the period of abduction the house of the informer was isolated by a terrible and intimate silence as though the inhabitants were dead from plague. The house was haunted by the knowledge of the victims' difficult confessions, the tentative and halting descent into a narrative of betrayal. The army moved in slowly on their bodies. They were studied from a distance, the location circled by helicopters. The official justification for these exercises was that the area had to be checked for booby traps but there were elements of mourning involved; the careful movement of torches among trees after dusk, the distant beat of rotors, a sense in the air that instinctual patterns of loss were being exhibited.

Following Hacksaw's confession Victor was re-arrested and charged with the O'Neill killings. Herbie was confident he could persuade McGrath to name Victor at his trial. Victor was assigned a cell on D-wing in the Crumlin Road. Most of the other inmates knew Victor. He no longer had to project menace. He joked with them, asked about wives and girlfriends.

The prison building was a geometric expression of rigorous morality. There were tiered levels of wrought-iron catwalks, ornate routines of containment and humiliation. With its corridors and long perspectives it seemed a place for penitents moving in procession, chanting the mournful stanzas of their contrition.

Many of the prisoners on the wing were young and demoralized, queuing for Valium outside the pharmacy on weekdays, treasuring the plastic capsules as symbols of a secret brotherhood with tendencies towards oblivion. It was easy for Victor to assert his superiority. Within a month his cell had become the centre of the wing. He was at home in closed societies with their stringent and predictable codes of behaviour. At this time he felt at his most powerful. His life was a thing hedged with magic and the possibilities of renewal. Alone in the dark he listened to messages tapped on the hot-water pipes, signals aimed at no one in particular, circling the prison and going unheard in empty boiler rooms and roof cavities, a subdued and confidential tapping long into the night.

Once a week Victor was interviewed by Herbie. The detective made Victor curious. He gave the impression of a man at the limit of endurance, possessed of an exhausting knowledge. He questioned Victor for hours about obscure incidents: a fight outside a pub, the theft of a car, a suicide found in the Lagan. His interrogations were conducted in perplexed digressions.

'You are in a strange position Victor.'

'What are you on about?'

'What does it feel like to be in the same prison as the man who is going to give evidence against you?'

'Nobody's giving no evidence against me.'

'Hacksaw's doing a pretty good imitation of somebody's going to give evidence against you, Victor. Must be a lonely position. I saw him the other day. Blood seems to have drained from his face. Comes out of that cell like something dug from the ground.'

'I wouldn't take a pension to be in that fucker's shoes.'

'I bet you stare at him in the dining hall, sitting at a table on his own with the head down in case he meets somebody's eyes. Do you know what sensory deprivation is? You end up floating in a tank. You can't hear or see nothing. Nobody can stick it for more than an hour or two. They start to have hallucinations. There's madness under the skin but you know that, Victor. That's what I want Hacksaw to feel in his cell. I want him to have visions. Spinning bright lights when he shuts the eyes. Staring out the window at the sun till it becomes a wheel of fire in the fucking wilderness? Because that's when I reckon he's going to break down and name you, am I right?'

'All I know is I feel sorry for him.'

'How come you feel sorry for him? Is it because he's alone? Because his family's been ostracized by now? That they've got McGrath is a tout painted on their gable wall and got blankets soaking in the bath in case somebody bucks a petrol bomb through the living-room window in the middle of the night?'

'I don't know nothing about that,' Victor said, leaning back in his chair and closing his eyes dreamily. 'I feel sorry for the cunt because he's already dead.'

'Dead's something you'd know about Victor, am I right?'

'You don't catch Victor Kelly out that easy, Herbie,' Victor said, smiling at him.

Dorcas visited. When Victor was brought into the room she was already seated at the other side of the table like some unrelenting protagonist. He could feel her studying him as he crossed the room, alert for weight loss, signs of internal struggle, taking inventory of her son. He would sit down and light a cigarette before he spoke.

'Well, ma,' he'd say, 'anything strange or startling?'

'You don't look yourself Victor. When will it end?'

'Listen ma, take her easy. It's not so bad in here. I'm doing a lot of reading and all.'

'Victor, I wrote a rake of letters. I wrote to the police about their error. I wrote to the papers about the innocence of my son and the low state of justice in this country.'

'You don't have to do things like that, ma.'

'I done it and I may as well not have done it for all they're interested. They had this photo of the mayor at a flower show in all the papers the other day while there's scandal all the time under their noses. It's a case of hand in glove, Victor.'

'I read your stars for you this morning. They said to exercise caution in financial matters this month. They said somebody close would surprise you.'

'Meaning maybe your da will open his mouth for once and talk to me. Honest to God, Victor, you'd think the man was swore to silence on the Bible, that it was damnation to let a word escape. I should of never married him. He's like a silent allegation of blame or deceit in the house. You'd not be as lonely in a prison cell.'

'I'm not lonely, ma. I've got a lovely big blondie girl up in the cell so I have.'

'I can't understand that McGrath turning tout on you. If you'd seen my face when they told me it was a mask of disbelief. You never done nothing to turn his hand against you like that. Loyalty to friends is a quality in you like your mother.'

'I got these books out of the library here, ma, that explain Hacksaw. Some people is drove to lies. I can't explain it, like they have to make themselves important. They're small people. They lack convictions in their life like I've got. They invent things and say things like they went out with some famous woman or shot somebody when they haven't. I started work in the hospital here and I have these conversations with the doctor about it.'

'That's good. Talk with a doctor. I wish you'd quit going around them clubs and all when you get out.'

'Ma, I can't explain it. I think deeply here. I got a job to finish. The Catholics in this town think they can just take over, the IRA and all. Walk all over you if you let them.'

'Your da has me drove mad, Victor.'

'Wait till I tell you something about this place, ma.'

Sooner or later during the visit their conversations began to diverge. It gave Dorcas a helpless feeling, herself talking about one thing and Victor talking about another. It was as if Victor was already back in his cell and she was back turning the key of the house which always seemed vast and echoing after her absence, a cavernous depot for the storage of marital silences.

Victor began to work in the prison pharmacy. First of all he was just pushing a trolley around, giving out prescriptions. He had a white coat and joked with the patients.

'Here's Doctor Victor. Got the pills to heal your ills.'

Waiting for the prescriptions to be made up he would sit in a corner of the pharmacy. It was a place that seemed replete with possibilities. There were gleaming instruments, locked drug cabinets made of green metal and rows of small prescription bottles. It was a place which made death and illness verifiable qualities, something measured in pipettes and remote from the human frame. It seemed possible that they could make you die in extraordinary ways here, deft and calculated modes of extinction.

The doctor in fact never spoke to Victor. He was a small man who became involved in small tasks — polishing his glasses, arranging the surface of his desk in neat formations of records and prescriptions. This was his first act every morning. It was a fixing of the boundaries that Victor understood, an act of seclusion.

There were medical textbooks on a shelf below one of the drug cabinets which Victor would open at random. He was drawn to words he could not understand. Prophylaxis. Descriptions of states he could not imagine. Toxaemia, pyrogenesis. They seemed to him like the separate volumes of a book of transformation. There were other books there on the forms of mental illness. Victor concealed some of these under his shirt and brought them back to his cell where he kept them hidden. When he opened them at night they seemed like a description of a huge building beyond his comprehension. He had frightening thoughts of dimly lit vaults, miles of passageway, directions indicated by strange inscriptions. He dreamed of crypts where the unnamed case histories in the book were sunk in thousand-year sleep. Narcolepsy. His reading was slow and painful but he persisted. He admired willpower. He sat at the small table in the cell although it would have been more comfortable on the bed. The position of the body was important. He began to understand that reading required rigour from the body, acts of piety and self-denial. He read until his joints were stiff and his hands were cold and difficult to manipulate. He used his finger to follow the words and his lips moved to invoke each syllable. There was hidden power here, the voice raised to an incantatory pitch.

Victor wanted to get into the drug cabinets in the dispensary. He consulted a prisoner on the ordinary wing who was doing time for housebreaking who told him that old-fashioned safes and cabinets were much easier to force open from behind. When the doctor was doing his weekly clinic Victor moved the cabinet out from the wall to find that the back was secured by four small screws. It was a matter of seconds for him to remove the top two and bend the panel back. He reached in and removed a small jar, taking a quick glance at the contents before he slipped it into his pocket. It contained purple and white capsules which seemed to possess the necessary colours and dimensions of the serious drug capable of producing fundamental change in the organism.

Later that night Victor examined the bottle in his cell. The drug was called dexidrine. Victor couldn't believe it. It proved that he was lucky. Dexidrine was one of the drugs that McClure had mentioned to him. Blow your fucking brains out, he had said. Carry the head clean off you, leave you speeding out of the mind for two days. Victor held the capsule up to the light and the coloured grains inside shifted. It had a kind of internal animation, an authoritative feel in the hand. He imagined the drug rushing to his head and the emphatic glint of its crystals in the brain.

A week afterwards PO Matt McCulla was on duty in the lookout above the recreation yard. It was January and McCulla could see his breath drifting across the beam of the arc light beside him. He had his collar over his ears and his cap pulled low over his eyes. He had the universal stance of men on guard duty in watch-towers, border huts, unheated sentry-boxes. Men staring into pine forests and frozen wastes, watching the dark as though pledged to it.

McCulla sensed movement from the prison building behind him and turned. He saw a man lowering himself out of a third-storey window. A rope of knotted sheets dangled below him and he began to move slowly down the blankets, his face pressed closely against the brickwork as though it was an eroded text worthy of scrutiny. The end of the rope was short of the ground and if the man managed to drop off he would still be trapped. Escape was impossible. But McCulla realized that if the man descended another six or seven yards they would be at eye-level ten feet apart. They would be required to hold something approaching a conversation, to acknowledge each other as men who encounter each other in a wilderness. McCulla opened his mouth to shout, but he had been standing alone in the darkness for four hours and his voice seemed to have absented itself into the night, so that what came out was hoarse and alien, something directed from the fringes of a mob, a phrase of incitement.

Victor released his grip on the wall and allowed the rope to rotate so that he was looking down on McCulla. He was feeling exultant, suspended from the roof of his known world. He could see the shipyard and the city hall, traffic in motion, lights on the slopes of the mountains and the black water of the lough where the light ceased. It seemed that he could see how the city operated, that at its heart there was a set of mechanical principles, requirements to be fulfilled, and that they were within his grasp. He had taken two capsules of dexidrine an hour earlier, feeling its effects first as a kind of feral wariness, an impeccable state of alert in which he felt capable of detecting sounds beyond the range of the human ear. This was followed by a restless desire for activity when he began to knot together the blankets and sheets from his bed then let them out of the window.

Hanging there he could see the screw's white face below him. He felt like a piece of something icy and brilliant. He knew that if he attempted to escape he would succeed in a series of hairs-breadth calculations. He imagined it in the papers. Daring breakout. Fugitive from justice. But he knew that he had to deal with Hacksaw. McCulla watched in silence as Victor climbed back towards the window.

ten

Sundays in the city were still and vacant with flat grey skies or watery sunshine. It was the silence of the empty quarter, the uplifted quivering palm, the silent howl. In the morning congregations gathered outside churches and meeting halls then dispersed as if their acts of worship were a preliminary to greater assembly, a preparation towards some fervent communal act of expiation. Ryan's impression of this was reinforced by the long Sunday afternoons when it seemed that the population had deserted the streets and gathered dramatically on a hillside outside the city, hushed and expectant.

There had been no further knife killings and he had been avoiding Coppinger. They passed each other in the lobby with no sign of recognition. There was dark talk about the circles that Coppinger was moving in. He had become a centre of rumour and his actions were discussed with the kind of hostility normally reserved for immigrant Indians and Chinese in the city. See how dirty. Ryan thought that Coppinger had achieved the burning belief of a despised prophet. His reports, precise and factual, were frequently rejected. There was something frightening about them. They read as if they had been stripped down and ordered according to an unimaginable necessity. They had the dry powdery feel of bones dried in the sun.

The bars in the city were closed on a Sunday. It was only possible to get a drink in a club or in some of the hotels. Ryan took a taxi across town to the York Hotel on Botanic Avenue where he rapped on the front door with a coin. He waited for a few minutes, then a man in a white shirt came to the door and scrutinized him through the glass. He unlocked the door silently and held it open. Ryan realized that there had been a time when he would not have passed this type of examination. He had somehow acquired the psychic credentials of the drinker, the sad, proclaiming spirit.

There were four or five men at the bar. Heavy velvet curtains were drawn across the windows and the lights were on. Ryan liked the atmosphere, redolent of self-forgiveness and gracious moments of reprieve.

The man in the white shirt moved behind the bar where he stood waiting. Ryan ordered a whiskey. Turning, he realized that Coppinger had been standing at the bar beside him. Concealed by the practised stance of anonymity. Ryan noticed how his eyes had changed. They seemed to be a sniper's eyes, deeply sunk, accustomed to range and distance.

'It's a funny thing about these city centre bars,' Coppinger said, 'the way they're neutral zones. People take a break from the practice of bitterness. They're protective about the status of the place.'

'An element of sanctuary,' Ryan suggested, 'weapons piled at the door.'

'Could be. There must have been a declaration, a decree handed down from some obscure council.'

'Something I keep noticing coming through the city centre on a Sunday is wee old men standing on street corners. Every corner has one. They talk to you when you pass them. They're the only people about. They make a point of sharing reminiscences with you.'

Ryan stopped. He realized that Coppinger and himself had always talked like this, exchanging observations about the city, developing small themes and drawing them out to their limits. It was an attempt to create new levels, to resist the city's definition of itself as violent, divisive, pitiful.

He knew that there were also depths of parody in these

conversations, a sideshow for good-humoured crowds at the place of execution.

'I was wondering,' he said hesitantly, 'did you hear anything more about the knife killings?'

'Nothing.'

'Do you think it was some kind of aberration?'

'What do you mean?'

'I'm not sure. An enthusiastic amateur or something.'

'What about O'Neill's then, that some sort of aberration?'

'Happens all the time. Your classic armed robbery gone wrong. I can see the statement now. "Guns started going off, I just pulled the trigger." Suspect begins to weep with genuine fear and bewilderment. No one knows how it got to the point of guns going off and bodies on the floor. They never really meant to kill anybody.'

'You don't believe that.'

'Somebody might have got carried away.'

'Shite. The word is that somebody's squealed, made a statement but refused to name people, and from what I hear of that statement nobody fucking panicked. Anyhow if you don't want to pursue it just forget it.'

'I want to pursue it. I can't forget it.' The words were out of Ryan's mouth before he realized that he had spoken them, and he was aware of a pressing fear.

'You look shook,' Coppinger said.

'I can't explain it. It's like you close your eyes and see the whole thing in flashback.'

'You been down at the magistrates' court lately? They bring these wee bastards in. Seventeen, eighteen years old. They've already spilled the beans and you get this detective reading out their statement. They all say the same thing. "It was like a film." "It was like something out of the pictures." Like they're not really shooting anybody.'

'They're absolving themselves of blame. Like as soon as they run away the victim's going to stand up, dust himself off.'

'I don't reckon that's it. I think that's the way they remember it. Frame by frame. The look of terror on the victim's face. The pleading eyes. Throwing up their arms in slow motion as the bullet enters. It's all got to do with memory. It's the way you remember sex or violence.'

It was the way Ryan remembered the night that finished his marriage. One of those long drinking evenings, moving through the strata of the marriage with a kind of calm professionalism. Reminiscence, speculation, resentment — these were the zones of marginal yield, half-heartedly indulged until they reached the rich vein of betrayal and hostility. She would often decide to leave the flat then, depriving Ryan of a focus for his anger. She ran to bus depots, railway stations. Once she rang Ryan from the airport, drunk and weeping. There was something in large, echoing public buildings which satisfied her. She was calmed by place-names being spoken over a Tannoy, the solace of destinations. When he drove to the airport that morning she was sitting on a bench listening to announcements of departures and arrivals with her eyes closed and a smile on her face, sunk in some private rapture which lasted until they got back to the house in Stranmillis where she went to bed and was asleep in seconds, still smiling.

But what he remembered now was the night he tried to stop her leaving, following her into the bathroom where she was holding her hair back with one hand and tying an elastic band around it with the other.

'Fuck're you going?' he said. He always felt intimidated by her acts of preparation in front of the mirror, her lips pursed, as though the body in the mirror belonged to someone else who was teaching a sequence of feminine gestures which must be followed precisely.

'I'm only going out for a walk. Go to bed.'

'You always walk off. Spoil a good argument.'

'You always,' she mocked.

'Never fucking stay.' He felt uncouth and mumbling. She belonged somewhere with this white light, taut and estranged, of formica and porcelain. He had a sudden vision of the next day. The shame and sense of amnesty. Mean what you said? The contrite words, grateful subterfuges, promises. Both accepting the reprieve, waking late and dehydrated, drinking pints of water in bed. Forgiveness.

'You never,' she said, walking past him out of the bathroom. 'You always and you never. You shit. You fuck. Pitiful fucking you. Pitiful fuck.'

He hit her under the eye, her head striking the doorframe. She slid on to the floor and held her face in her hands. After a long time she turned her head to look at him. They said nothing. It needed time to realign themselves to the event. A moment to be replayed, savoured, not spoken of.

'Where does that leave us?'

'I think the man we're looking for is doing time somewhere. He's either on remand or he's been interned. The atmosphere is different somehow. It's like there's a variation in the rhythm, but the theme's going to re-emerge somewhere like something monstrous with kettledrums and all.'

'How come you're so fucking brainy Coppinger?'

'Piss off and order us a drink.'

They spent the rest of the afternoon in the bar locked into discussion of the knife killings and the O'Neill murders. Rumours were beginning to surface of paramilitary and British Intelligence involvement in a boys' home on the outskirts of the city. There was talk of politicians and senior civil servants being filmed or recorded in bed with teenage boys. No one seemed to know what uses this information was being put to. Coppinger claimed to know examples of nervous decision-making at high level which could only be put down to some potent encroachment on government thought. Ryan was sceptical of this, but Coppinger stressed the importance of rumour, the complex networks of dubious information that influenced every major event in the city. Riots, assassinations, the overnight flight of whole streets. Rumour was the means by which society confirmed its own worst suspicions. Dark mutterings. Coppinger said that it was always the primal response to instability. It was an essential factor in historical events, situations which lent themselves to powerful fictions: soothsayers, exhausted riders at the city gates with tales of strange happenings, signs and portents.

'You're probably thinking this is fanciful shit,' Coppinger said. 'Poor fucker's been out in the wilds so long his fucking porch light's gone out on him. But this is where we're looking for our man. We're not going to find this fucker asking questions on doorsteps. Excuse me, missus, but did you see a man walking down the street with a bloodstained knife in his mitt like. You got to get right to the source of all the rumours, the fear.'

'Besides,' he went on, 'you're supposed to be a journalist, how many things have you found out about him?'

'Fuck-all except what I read in the papers.'

'Exactly. Nobody knows what's going on. Everybody's got a different version. There's a heap of intelligence agencies got their fingers in the pie as well as the usual players. None of them co-operating and all of them spreading different versions of what's going on, spreading the story that suits them and not telling anybody else. When nobody's in control watch out my son.'

'So what do we do now?'

'Sit tight and wait for him to get out.'

'What if he's been put away for twenty years?'

'He hasn't.'

'Do you know something you're not letting on about?'

'It's not that, just a feeling you get from talking to people. I suppose if he'd been put away for a good long while people would be telling you more. You get the impression that they're not looking over their shoulder as much, but that it's a temporary thing. I tried going through the names of internees and remand prisoners but there's millions of the bastards. Don't worry, we'll know when he gets out. Give you something to look forward to.'

'There's a problem with waiting. By the time he gets out you and me'll probably not have any jobs any more.'

Both of them knew that they were in trouble at work. Coppinger because his copy was being rejected. Ryan because of missing days and arriving into work drunk or hung-over. He knew that his appearance had changed. He went for days without changing his shirt. There were stains on his trousers and jacket. He could detect pity from those at work. He felt as if he was experimenting with the concept of a man in disintegration, moving through the stages of personal neglect as if it were an exact science with observable phenomena of decay, nuances of futility.

There were other factors in their feeling of insecurity. Both of them were experiencing difficulty in defining their jobs. Somehow the state of civil unrest in the city had made them feel obsolete, abandoned on the perimeter of a sprawling technology of ruin. Coppinger said that he was experiencing a new species of information. Paramilitary organizations operating under cover names. Politicians issued ambiguous statements of condemnation. In court unidentified witnesses gave evidence from behind screens. The facts were equivocal and it had become impossible to pin down responsibility. Each time Coppinger wrote up a killing he felt that the report acquired implications which he had not put there. It hinted at something covert, unexplained, dissatisfying. Several journalists had been shot, many had been threatened.

The bar filled quietly over the afternoon. No one raised their voice. There was an air of serious business, transactions being carried out in the medium of comfort, mercy. Ryan was reminded of funerals, the soft instructions whispered by undertakers, the murmurs of condolence. They were both drinking whiskey.

Night had fallen when they left the bar. They walked towards Shaftsbury Square. There was no one else about. A Belisha beacon flashed at a pedestrian crossing. There was the sound of a helicopter coming from the North of the city, a melancholic stirring of the air, dark, hinting at calamity.

At the bottom of Dunegall Pass they were stopped by an army foot patrol. One of the soldiers asked for their names and addresses and their destination. The others crouched in doorways scanning the rooftops, their faces doubtful, as if the buildings themselves, the form and structure of the city, were untrustworthy, possessed of a dubious topography which required constant surveillance.

The soldier taking their names spoke in a low Scottish accent. He transcribed their names carefully, asking each man to spell his surname. He had difficulty with the addresses so that they had to correct him several times. Ryan had seen this before — people in trouble taking infinite care over spellings as if they were eager to implicate themselves. Coppinger started to discuss the upcoming Glasgow Rangers game with the soldier. The soldier's answers were short. He had been in the city long enough to recognize a breach of propriety, a deviation from the careful hostility which was supposed to accompany such interviews. Coppinger had abandoned the terse recognized forms. The soldier shifted his rifle to hold it across his chest. Ryan saw a threat in the gesture but Coppinger continued to speak urgently, his words acquiring the imperative cadences of a football commentator, the voice pitched above the roar of the crowd, striving to make the audience identify with events on the field, the floodlit and solitary exertions, the last-minute transcendence of suffering. The soldier began to swear at Coppinger. Ryan stepped in between them and Coppinger stopped talking, hanging his head and breathing lightly. Another member of the patrol across the street whistled and raised his arm at the other.

They had spent too long in one place. They had a schedule to follow. Streets to be crossed at a crouching run. Nervous drunk men to be questioned. With a last angry look at Coppinger the soldier turned and followed the others down the street.

Ryan looked at Coppinger who held out one hand, asking for respite before he spoke as if he was winded. Eventually he straightened.

'Just keep your eyes and ears open for news. And go back to that wife of yours. You should never have let her kick you out in the first place. Now fuck off home and leave me be.'

He turned abruptly and walked off down Dunegall Pass, a short figure in a brown coat moving confidently under street-lights. Ryan contrasted it to his own furtive gait, the walk of a man who was an accomplice to things he did not understand.

As he walked home Ryan realized that he had not heard Coppinger's address. He had a vague memory of a street name, one of the small streets off the Shankill perhaps, but he couldn't be certain. It was a mark of Coppinger's identification with the city. It was common to be stopped on the street and asked for your name and address. Inhabitants of the city were adept at deciphering the clues to religion and status contained in an address. Sectarian killers worked on that basis, picking up their victims according to the street they lived in. Your address was a thing to be guarded as if the words themselves possessed secret talismanic properties. Your name was replete with power and hidden malevolence.

When he got back to the flat Ryan opened a bottle of whiskey and sat in the front room with the lights off. The room was full of Victorian furniture. Heavy pieces with the mandatory gleam of serious purpose. They were declarations of the sombre mercantile ethic which had constructed the houses in this part of the city.

He pulled his chair in front of the window and reached for the telephone. He dialled Margaret's number. As it rang he realized that she would see the call as being in character. Drunk and alone, nursing obscure wounds, he would call her. Towards the end he had realized that she expected to be disappointed in him. It was the way she protected herself, and she required him to conform to the role. She detected sins of unpunctuality, lack of commitment, silence. It gave her the power of forgiveness and she dispensed measured quantities of absolution. She expected him to fail at small missions. To turn up punctually at the wrong location. It was a method they had developed of avoiding the fundamentals.

'Hello?' Her voice was sleepy but prepared to be alarmed. They shared the same dread of phone calls late at night with their overtones of sudden death.

'Hello?' she repeated, a note of panic entering her voice. He imagined her sitting up in bed, settling the blankets over her knees, pushing her hair out of her eyes in a rapid sequence of familiar gestures. Arrangements in the immediate world designed to meet the unknown.

'Ryan, you bastard,' she said. He realized the reason he had called her was to find out if she was with someone. He was listening to her words for an apportioning of sound, some part of her voice relinquished to a figure in the bed beside her.

'This is you, Ryan. This is really you.' Her voice implied that he was doing something which had been done before, better, by someone else. He replaced the receiver with the feeling that something in his life had remained familiar and intact.

eleven

Often Heather would wake to find McClure sitting on the edge of her bed wearing a fixed grin like something placed there during the night by malicious hands, a crude idol of warning and malediction. Since Victor had been arrested she had felt increasingly possessed by McClure. She found that even her speech had begun to imitate his sinister drawl with its stylized note of foreboding. He would take her out drinking, then give her a new name for the night. He would invent an occupation for himself. On particular nights they were a conservatory salesman from Larne and his placid wife. They sat in carpeted lounge bars where a man played waltz tunes on an electronic organ and exhorted the audience to sing along to sentimental songs that left Heather with a lump in her throat feeling bereft. They held long conversations with old couples sitting beside them, conversations full of the complicity of the married, sly jokes about starting families, about the neglect visited by grown children, rueful jokes about growing old, about grand-children and the longings of the elderly. Afterwards McClure cursed them with violent and consuming bitterness.

One morning he presented her with two small capsules and a glass of water.

'What's them for?'

'Tuinol. Get them down your neck.'

'What are they for?'

'They're for your head. Your fucked-up head.'

She took the capsules from his outstretched hand and

swallowed them. She turned away from him and began to doze. When she woke she was lying on her back. The bed-clothes had been lifted away and her nightdress was around her neck. McClure was standing beside the bed masturbating with his right hand. His teeth were clenched and there were flecks of spittle in the corners of his mouth. She regarded him with massive, barbiturate indifference. The darkened room was permeated with an atmosphere of ordeal. Turning her head away she had an impression of time suspended, an interval of mourning.

The Saturday night parties continued, but she began to occupy a different role. McClure cracked open benzedrine inhalers in the kitchen then moved from group to group with his teeth showing. Mad disciple of perdition and loss. Heather drank little and sat on the outside of groups listening to their conversations until she detected the dark, fluting tones of despondence and apprehension. Towards the morning she sought out those sitting on their own where she would engage them in soft talk using words of lucid memory. First love. Words handled until they had acquired a dull shine, the valid texture of familiar truth. Home, gentle, wife. She came across a young policeman sitting on the toilet with his trousers around his ankles and his service revolver on his bare knees and talked to him for three hours about his early life. Where were you born? What school did you go to? Evocations in resilient miniature. The man closed his eyes and rocked backwards and forwards reciting the history of the place he came from. A small town childhood touched on. Parents, aunts, uncles produced for her inspection like a series of painfully unearthed ancestral fragments.

In the first weeks she had known Victor they would always leave towards the end of the parties. They would walk across Wellington Park and Chlorine Gardens then climb over the fence beside the university sports centre in the Botanic Gardens. Victor was awkward among the flowerbeds and tended paths. The park contained unfamiliar symmetries. The palm house, the bandstand. Things accumulated over years had been arranged into these composed and satisfactory events. For Victor they lacked the criteria of route and destination.

One morning they came across a group of youths lying on the grass beside the bandstand. The ground around them was strewn with empty cider bottles and brown paper bags smeared with industrial Evo-stic. They didn't look up when Victor and Heather approached them. All three faces wore incalculable expressions. They seemed to have drawn deeply on inner resources to achieve a set task. They did not protest when Victor sat down beside them and removed a half-empty bottle of Strongbow from one of their hands. He drank from the bottle with an air of satisfaction, as though he had recognized their discovery of a hidden destination in the park.

She was reminded of this in September when McClure took her to Lady Dixon's park to look for psilocybin mushrooms. He showed her how to recognize the mushroom's toxic skullcap in the grass. During the first hour she found none. McClure came over to her impatiently. He told her to narrow her eyes, find the range. If she was starving, he said, she would find them. If they were hidden mines. She wasn't picking fucking daisies. She had to bring urgency to the task.

She began to spot small groups of mushrooms immediately afterwards, bent over and scanning the ground, suddenly sensitive to the small uneasy presences in the wet grass. She had never studied the ground this closely before. She moved from patch to patch without thinking, as if following some ancient track, an hallucinatory spore path, compelling but unemphatic. She did not know how long she had been doing this when she became aware of formal borders around her. Looking up she realized that she had wandered into the grounds of a big red-brick building. She felt a sudden sense of fear, the hairs rising on the back of her neck as if there was a large, feral presence nearby, watching her from the trees, something light-footed and insatiable. She straightened up and looked around wildly. She could not see anything. Then she turned towards the building. Its long, ground-floor window was lined with old people who were staring at her. They were only ten feet away and she could make them out clearly. The wheelchairs, the aluminium walking frames, legs wrapped in elastic bandages, the medieval eye patches, liver spots, uncontrollable shaking. The window seemed like a museum case clustered with exhibits of human disorder. She felt trapped in that calm and hopeless regard, brought before a tribunal placed beyond the range of human complaint, wielding a comfortless jurisdiction granted only to those who lived in the proximity of death.

She told McClure about it in the car on the way back down the Malone Road. He laughed. She wondered if he had somehow arranged for her to be in the vicinity of the old people's home. When he had stopped in front of her flat he turned to her.

'Hacksaw won't testify against Victor.'

'You sound very sure of yourself.'

'I am.'

'The fucking bigshot. How does this happen?'

'I got a message into Victor. He knows what to do. There's plenty working in the prison that's sympathetic. The rest can be made sympathetic.'

'Victor never told me about anything of this.'

'That's because you never go and see him.'

'I couldn't bear it. I write to him. Besides, there's his precious mother takes up all the visits.'

'Anyhow. All going well you'll see him soon. You just try and keep it warm for him.'

Darkie continued to call to the flat, and she had trouble finding the words to resist his advances. She felt that there must be a word or a phrase which possessed the exact conclusive property. She also suspected that he watched the flat.

'You've changed,' he would say, watching her move around the room. The deserted lover's complaint, a centuries-old cry of lament that seemed to involve an element of lost nationhood. He spoke to her sparingly, choosing each sentence carefully for its qualities of misgiving.

'What's happened to you, Heather?'

'What do you mean, what's happened to me? Nothing's happened to me.'

'You used to be different. Not so serious or nothing. It's like you've been took over.'

'I can't help it, Darkie. I went and fell for somebody.'

'They're only using you.'

'That's what men do. Use you.'

'You don't know what you're getting into. Control is what they're after. Chew you up and spit you out. You look different even.'

'I know what I'm getting into. What do you mean, look different?'

'You look like something that somebody owns. A jacket, a shoe, something to wear.'

'A shoe, Darkie?'

'You look like something that somebody's owned for a long time, knows exactly what to do with. Something getting a bit worn.'

'What kind of shoe, Darkie? A stiletto? A slingback? What do I wear myself with?'

'Someday he's going to step out of you. Like, I've wore this long enough.'

'I'll get myself reheeled. A shoe, you prick.'

'You never knew when you were well off.'

They had the same argument every time. The responses were handed down from argument to argument. Accusation and counter-accusation. Exasperation. Ceremonial exchanges at the gates of desire.

The argument would last an hour at most before it would peter out, tribute paid to the smallness of its sentiment. Heather would join Darkie in the living-room, wearing a dressing gown, hair unwashed. It was part of a policy of careful disarray calculated to make him feel privileged. The cracked nail polish and period pains symptoms of the inept and needy self.

Darkie understood. He moved warily around her, making tea in the kitchen and speaking in low tones as if he saw her bathed in a favoured light. These were among her precious memories; the day fading, the candour of late afternoon, holding hands and speaking of hopes they had cherished for themselves when the city seemed spacious and candid, not the lost place it was now, the scene of a great crime in the hearts of men to be picked over for clues as they did now with sad forensic talk.

During these talks it seemed to her that Darkie had receded. It was as if he was aware of his own impending demise and regarded it as a weighty private matter requiring careful planning and the advice of friends. He had stopped distributing the pamphlets. There was no need for them any more, he said. The violence had started to produce its own official literature. Mainly hardbacks, with the emphasis on the visual. Photographs of bombs at the moment of detonation, riot scenes, men in balaclavas displaying heavy machine-guns, burnt-out vehicles, moments of numbness and shock. There was the inevitable photograph of the civilian victim. Darkie was haunted by the idea that the photograph was always of the same man taken from different angles. He brought Heather a sheaf of photos clipped from different books. Look, he said, the same shabby grey suit, the ill-matched socks and pale shins revealed by trouser legs which weren't long enough. The same uneven pavement. The same sensation that the man had been working all his life to achieve this position, this carefully contrived attitude of death something he had aspired to from birth. His growing-up, his marrying, his poverty were all minor adjustments, details he had added to give authenticity and stature to this position, the hands and face pressed to the ground in a fierce clinging gesture as though he was hanging on to the side of a building. Darkie wondered how he had died. Shot running away from a checkpoint, a hit from a high-velocity rifle aimed from a block of flats, chased into the street and shot point-blank from close range. Another thing, Darkie said, you never see this man's face. The photographer had gone to great lengths to avoid the possibility of identification. Neither was the man named in any of the books. To Darkie it all pointed to the amateur status of this death. The limbs were arranged with a touching awkwardness, a collection of graceless angles. Examined closely there was something apologetic about this dying. Perhaps this was why you were not shown the face, Darkie said. Perhaps you would see a self-deprecating grin, a small plea for forgiveness.

Big Ivan and Willie Lambe came to visit her as well. She could see that they were lost without Victor and abashed in her presence. She told McClure they always looked as if they were about to wee themselves. Cannon fodder, McClure called them, then said be nice to them, they might be useful.

They would come in and sit on the edge of the sofa. Big Ivan looked miserable and contrite. His eyes kept travelling to his big hands as if they were something uncouth which had followed him in. They took their duty as Victor's mates seriously, and visiting Heather while Victor was inside was an act of duty. But she could see that for Big Ivan especially it involved a facing-up to inner terrors. She teased him with this. Got a girlfriend yet Ivan? He would shake his head and fall silent, conveying the impression of a colossal yearning, a mute, cavernous pain.

She had a sense of the huge faith they had invested in Victor. A devotion almost religious in its intensity. They carried it about with them like a relic, age-blackened and hedged with awe. She knew that she had to treat them with caution. There was a chance that they would regard her as a threat; a big woman whose gestures conveyed an impression of sexual appetite. They avoided touching her and brought her presents of drink and cheap perfume you could buy in the Cornmarket which they left on the sideboard as though they were offerings intended to appease. She was taken aback when Willie told her one day that his mother wanted to meet her. Willie didn't seem surprised. It seemed that he regarded them both as capricious and potent deities.

Willie picked her up early on a Saturday morning. It was raining. There were women with umbrellas and scarves moving from doorway to doorway. Areas of heat and light. Looking at them made her think about standing in the doorway of the Mourne bakery when she was young. Men pushing noisy metal trolleys, transformed by the smell of bread and their white uniforms into careful tenders, men that might cry easily. Willie pulled up outside a small terraced house.

'Door's open,' he said. 'Just open it and walk in. I'll hold on here for you.'

Heather ran from the car to the front door. She knew that Willie's mother would be waiting for her in the front parlour. These houses always had a preserved and ordered room kept for greeting guests. The household's most approved objects arranged and polished to give a sense of occasion. The protocol of interiors.

She paused in front of the door, gathering herself. The meeting had suddenly taken on the air of being long-awaited. She felt a shiver at the thought of Willie's mother weighing events and deciding on the auspicious moment.

Mrs Lambe was sitting at a low table beside the window with her face held in profile by the rainy light. Here is a woman proud of her skin, was Heather's first thought. She knew she was meant to notice the fine grain which said this is a woman who has taken precautions over the years and has learned to appreciate the cleansing lustre of selfishness.

'The hair is wrong,' the woman said, looking at Heather. Heather said nothing. She could understand an old woman sustained by observing the flaws of others.

'When I was your age I could sit on my hair,' Mrs Lambe continued, making a gesture with her left hand which encouraged Heather to examine the photographs which covered every flat surface in the room. Evidence amassed of the crime done to her by the years.

'The dress is not right either. You must recognize the requirements of the full figure. You need a dress loose on the bosom, nipped at the waist.' She leaned forward and touched Heather lightly above her hipbone. It was only accomplished by frugal movements like an exercise in an uneasy science of conservation. There was an awareness of weak points, hairline cracks, fatigue.

'Here is a framed photograph of my husband and me,' Mrs Lambe said, directing Heather's gaze towards the frame nearest to her. Heather recognized it as a holiday photograph taken by a commercial photographer. There were always two or three of these men on the promenade during the summer when she was young. Their work always filled her with a kind of sorrow. The pictures seemed to be developed by a secret process which imbued them with the sad facts of the photographer's profession. The smiling faces of the subjects took on a harried, transient air. Nameless migrants waiting to embark. The photographer himself seemed to be looking beyond them towards a lonely and disappointed old age.

'Mr Lambe sung lead vocal in a band. The man had such a voice he could have had any girl he wanted. He picked me as the one he was going to be unfaithful to for the rest of his life.' The statement was made tiredly. Heather imagined her alone in her bed rehearsing these practised ironic phrases and the cracked, bitter laughter. Heather examined the man's face, but the telling detail was in the way he was dressed. The Brylcreemed hair, the blazer and flannels. Here was a man who would fly into a rage over a stain. The ultimate knife-edge crease, the dreamed glow of polished shoes. These were the things that contained all he wished to know of the world. A wardrobe-space, something portable. Not enough to fill all the rooms of a marriage. On his arm he had a pretty girl from the city, dressed to the nines and interchangeable with others who came in their season.

'Is he still alive?' Heather asked.

'Dead of cancer,' the old woman replied. 'He sung that song right.'

There was a silence in the room. The tick of a clock. The overflow of a gutter jammed with leaves. It was a carefully judged period of remission in which to contemplate the human residue.

'William was a late child. His head was too big. He did not speak at all until he was four years old. He sat with his big head like a dumbbell. I was near forty. The doctor warned me of consequences. Birth defects. Prolapse of the uterus. When he was six years old he stuck a compass into the face of another child. To see what would happen, I believe. There was talk of the courts.'

'I have always held that there is a want in him. Something in the eye that would lead a body to say here is someone that is not just right. That is the expectation in a late child. He left job after job, the last being as a filleter of fish. Since he begun to take the government's money I have developed a concern about the people he is running around with. He is like a dangerous thing in the wrong hands doing damage.'

'Victor looks after him, Mrs Lambe.'

'But you see what I mean. He is running round with imprisoned people.'

'Victor's only on remand. He never done nothing. It'll come out in court.'

'There's no smoke without fire, but I see you are took in also. I thought you had sense until I seen you walk in. William talked about you. You give him tea when he calls and perhaps advice, I thought. A girl who is aware. But the way you dress.

You treat your body as if it is goods. And slopping all over without a brassière. I thought someone I could trust was here. A woman to share confidences.'

Heather could feel the room suddenly charged with the woman's rage like something just beyond the range of the human ear, and realized that the furniture and photographs were arranged according to the dynamics of madness.

'I have to go now, Mrs Lambe.'

'You have something to do? Maybe it's to get into the back seat with William? I wouldn't do that. I believe there are things he would do on a woman's body. I hear on the wireless a woman's body found I ask myself, where was William? You might think to get yourself off easy young lady but you will discover grief with this gang of men. You will endure pain.'

When Heather got back to the car Willie was listening to the weather forecast, the announcer's voice striking notes of warning, low pressure and weather building without respite.

twelve

Victor was on the landing outside his cell talking to one of the screws. A red-faced man from Ballysillan or somewhere, Victor thought, one of those windy and resentful new estates with street kerbing painted red, white and blue and loyalist slogans on gable ends. He talked to Victor in a confidential way, like they were best friends.

'See me, I'm a man with the ear to the ground. I know what's going on. Fucking Catholics. Equal fucking housing, equal votes. Fuckers looking for Protestants out of their jobs, out of their houses. Breeding like rabbits and living off the dole, off people like me pays their taxes. They don't want to work. Their women carrying their bombs for them. Their women coming in here, objects concealed in the vagina.'

'Then there's the IRA in here. Walk around like they own the place with big talk about political status and all. A man like me knows a sell-out when he sees it.'

Victor was occupied with the problem of Hacksaw. He saw him every day in the canteen eating with the non-political prisoners. For fear of Victor no one spoke to him, but Victor stared at him every day, hoping to catch his eye. One day he did lift his face in Victor's direction but it seemed that he did not recognize him. His face was deeply etched and his eyes sunken. Victor noticed that his movements were refined and that he ate sparingly, sipping water. Talking to the screws he found out that two detectives who had been assigned to the case visited him every day and spent hours alone with him.

Leaving the cell they seemed like men who had endured rigours of the spirit.

The screws told Victor about an IRA prisoner who had nearly died after another had given him a bottle of lemonade containing paraquat. It showed a sense of imagination that Victor liked. He broke into the drug cabinet again looking for poison. He wanted to find cyanide. It sounded like something from the pictures. He thought of Bette Davis who was his mother's favourite. Passions seething beneath the surface. A glitter of madness in the eye with only the music giving it away, the fitful, nervy violins. Alone in a big house coming unhinged.

He knew that it was important to wait for the right moment. Everything falling into place and patterns forming, each step mapped in advance by the frugal and patient cartographer he carried in his head. In the meantime he worked on layouts and timing. Thirty seconds to get from the pharmacy to the landing, four minutes to cross the landings to Hacksaw's cell. Two sets of locked gates to get through. He felt like an athlete before the starter's pistol. Lean, prepared, monumental. The mind working towards the stark moment.

There were times when he sat on his own for hours on end just concentrating. Odd, sequestered periods.

The Ballysillan warder asked him casually one day if he knew McClure. Hiding his interest, Victor said that he did. The man nodded as if Victor had produced credentials. They talked about McClure briefly. It seemed that he had presented himself to the warder as someone devoted to combating Roman Catholic infiltration of government positions. Victor hid his smile of approval. It was McClure's style. Fitting himself to the secret fear, the hidden desire. Victor had seen him change his character four or five times a day, moving through a series of cold and dextrous personalities. McClure realized that people needed to confide those dangerous thoughts. They had to have a companion to guide them through the strange architecture of their loathing, someone to share its lonely grace.

There was a football match in the prison that Saturday, the warder said rapidly, a seven-a-side. The landings would be empty and the two warders who stood guard outside Hacksaw's cell would not be there. He would give Victor the two keys he needed for the landing gates and collect them again after the match. The man seemed surprised to hear himself speak these words. His look said that he was not the kind of man to see himself as part of a conspiracy. He was someone who spent his life complaining about plots, furtive designs, shadowy figures in offices. He saw himself as a man alone and hampered.

Victor spent the Friday night in the television room, which always filled up for the evening news. The inmates kept up with events in the city, avid for the images, but the camera had a way of finding strange angles on familiar scenes and often they had difficulty identifying a place, so that they had to struggle towards the moment of recognition.

'Twenty-four-year-old man wounded in sectarian attack on Lanark Way.'

Victor did not suffer from the same confusion. He mapped each incident in his head, working out approaches and escape routes.

'It is believed the gunmen made their escape on foot into the nearby Shankill area.'

One by one the men in the room would sit forward, eyes fixed on the screen. It seemed that this room was only one of many where men gathered in worried knots, anxious to understand.

Victor did not play football. Since the time his father had taken him to Linfield matches he had lost interest. He left the room when the others began to discuss the weekend matches, reading aloud from the sports pages. He wanted nothing to do with it. The theories of excellence, the lonely battles for fitness, the grim-faced managers. The whole struggle and glare of it was something he detested, its elements of public humiliation and short-lived triumph.

As he waited in the pharmacy he could sense the atmosphere of the match. It was being taken seriously in the prison. The players had been escorted from their cells an hour before kick-off carrying their kit. The other inmates touched them gently on the shoulder and urged them on with soft voices. There were gestures of compassion. Everyone wanted to touch the players as if their hands transferred sympathy like some healing liniment.

He looked at the pharmacy clock. It was five to three. He had the keys in his pocket like a secret. He would wait until the moment of kick-off when the crowd's attention would be unified and drawn towards the pitch. Something out there that distorted their faces. Something howling and powerful.

The warder had given him the keys earlier that morning. Palmed them in a film gesture that made Victor laugh. Like where did he think he was, Alcatraz? Victor pictured himself running across country, bursting through low scrub in prison workclothes, pursued by dogs through a stark, hunted landscape. He laughed again at the warder whose face was sweating and appalled at what he had just done and at the years of dread and fitful sleep stretching out from that moment.

Victor set off from the pharmacy. He had never seen the prison so empty, the landings deserted, the cell doors standing open as if each contained a small but ample instance of solitude, a carefully modelled prototype of human need. The sun coming in through skylights softened the edges of brick walls and doorframes and created shadows which seemed to correspond to his route. He crossed the landing and reached the first gate. He took the key from his pocket and fingered the oiled metal then slid it into the lock, enthralled by the blued chromium shaft, the deep complex colour and the softened, locking sound of the mechanism like a noise heard at the mind's edge by a man who dreams of a technology of enclosure.

When he entered the ordinary wing Victor was struck by the calm, as if the conditions here were different. It was a place to recognize limitations, to walk softly, work long hours at the patient craft of remorse. The fluorescent light seemed less harsh, and the building itself, its brickwork and aseptic paint, took on an aged and patient personality, tolerant of small passions. There was a forty-watt glow of easeful knowing.

Hacksaw's cell was the second from the end on the left-hand side. Victor moved slowly past the empty cells, looking into each. There were identical beds, steel-framed chairs with personal belongings and photographs neatly arranged. There was an artificial feel to it, a sense of preserved tradition, century-old interiors. Victor quickened his walk as he approached the end of the corridor. He adopted the old Dillinger gait, pacey and dangerous. A sweet-faced character in a double-breasted suit and shoes polished to death placing his foot on the threshold of Hacksaw's cell as though the exact angle of his body in the doorway had been planned months in advance.

Hacksaw was sitting on the edge of his bed, rocking, his eyes out of focus. Victor walked carefully towards him, moving slowly again, as if Hacksaw were a vessel that might spill.

There was dried mucus at the corners of Hacksaw's mouth. His skin was lifeless, shrunken into the hollows of his face. The rocking motion was insistent, demanding, a way of working himself into the deeper recesses of self. Victor had seen it before. Old men rocking on park benches. Poorly dressed women in the Labour Exchange. It had seemed to him a way of conveying the tidings of madness.

'Hacksaw.' Victor whispered the word. Hacksaw did not acknowledge him. Victor took a piece of paper from his pocket and smoothed it out.

'Listen, Hacksaw,' he said. 'I got this confession wrote out here to say you done them shootings on your own. You're going to sit down and copy it out and sign the fucker so you are.'

Hacksaw began to speak. His voice was weak at first, picking up as he continued.

'i been waiting on you, Victor. Many's the night I seen your face here in the window. Heard the wind in the trees.'

'Not so loud, Hacksaw. You wouldn't want anyone to hear this wee talk of ours.'

'Nobody hears nothing in here. I go a long way away from here these freezing nights, Victor. Going down Bedford Street, Tomb Street. Do you mind Frames? Me and Frames walking down the town. There's men from the police come here Victor, asking about you. I never told them nothing, Victor.'

'I know you didn't Hacksaw. All I want is for you to write out what you done and I'll leave you be.'

'I'm starting to forget things, Victor. I can't mind the words no more.'

'I've got the words here, a whole squad of words. All you got to do is copy them out.'

'I like this place here. It's quiet. No call for words at all. Put your words away, Victor.'

'All you got to do is copy them, Hacksaw.'

'No more words.'

'None after this. These is your last words and testament.'

In the end Victor had to hold his wrist as he copied the words of the confession, staring at the characters as if there was troubling news concealed within each shapely emerging form. When he had finished Victor had difficulty in reading it. The letters did not seem to bear any relationship to others he had seen. At first glance they did not appear to belong to any known language, but were something called up out of months of solitary confinement. It was a language of seclusion: plaintive, elegaic, lost.

Without realizing it Victor had spent almost an hour in the cell and it struck him that Hacksaw's confession would have to do. Hacksaw had resumed the rocking motion. Victor pushed him gently back on to the bed and lifted the pillow. Hacksaw barely resisted when Victor held it over his face.

'What do you feel now that Hacksaw's dead, son?'

'Don't feel nothing.'

'How'd you get into his cell?'

'Don't know what you're talking about, Herbie.'

'You've got a friend or two in here, Victor, am I right?'

'I'm the friendly sort so I am.'

'You got friends all right. Everybody with big faces on them, like I never done nothing. I just come up here to tell you, Victor, I know somebody's running you. Thing is you probably don't even know it and I like that, you want to know why? Don't try that fucking smile on me I'll ram it down your neck.'

'Take it easy there, Herbie, just fly her low.'

'You know why I'm glad someone's manipulating you, son? Because it means that one of these fine days you'll fuck up, you'll get a sudden rush of blood to the head, and they'll give you the old nut job, the big Victor Kelly turning up with a hole in the head.'

'That a fact?'

'I think it is.'

'Tell you what, I'll make you an offer.'

'What's that?'

'After the case comes up and I get off because poor old Hacksaw went and confessed I'll take you for a spin in the Capri.'

'I don't think so Victor.'

'Just for taking all this trouble.'

'I don't think so Victor. I don't think you'll be going for no spins nowhere. Want me to tell you why? Because there's a big detention order sitting in my office waiting for you soon as you walk out of that court. You're for the Kesh, Victor. Detention without trial, pleasure of the Secretary of State.'

'Fuck you, Herbie.'

'Glad to be of service, Victor.'

'You come here to tell me that, you can fuck off home now.'

'Tell us this, Victor, is there any truth in the rumours?'

'What rumours is these?'

'Rumours that your da's a Fenian, member of the Roman Catholic persuasion?'

thirteen

It was the first time Heather had been inside a courthouse. It was not what she expected. McClure told her that this was part of the mystery of courthouses. They are not what you expect. You look for authority in a courthouse, the exercise of prerogative. This is where the small acts of human deceit and betrayal are given latitude, where they should be played out in terms of motive, consequences. The dark benches, the archaic procedure designed to give you the drama you feel you are owed from your life, the feeling that you are acting on behalf of something great and shadowy.

Heather hadn't anticipated the room she was now in. It had the acoustic properties of a corridor. Instead of carefully pronounced phrases the lawyers mumbled and shuffled paper so that they were impossible to hear. They seemed to be inattentive to their client's cause. Something vital to the human condition was absent. There was nervous shuffling in the public gallery. It gave her the impression of a system close to collapse, with comic possibilities when you were looking for the dignity of ruined lives. She realized that it was just another of those buildings that government provided to contain people's disappointment.

McClure was sitting beside her, enjoying himself. He was wearing one of his grins. She did not have to speak to him to interpret it. Malice accomplished. He had pointed Dorcas out to her as they entered, pointing in such a way that Dorcas knew she was being looked at and why. Her son's slut, a bad feeling which Heather knew that she would cling to as an accessible hatred in the middle of all these lawyers with their air of knowing who was to blame. The two women were ten yards apart but the space between them was charged with grievance. It was the kind of familial rancour that McClure had a nose for. Heather had the urge to go over to the small woman in the tweed coat with gnarled leather buttons. To touch her shoulder and read in her face those things which addressed Victor.

Victor had spoken to her about Dorcas frequently. He always referred to her in sentimental terms and sent her cards with pink hearts. Sentiment was the way he made sense of his mother. She had noticed how men were drawn to the small adaptable emotions and the way they avoided whole areas of suffering, the barren tracts at the edge of love picked over by women.

When they brought Victor into the courtroom she barely recognized him. It wasn't that he had physically changed, but he seemed somehow to be transformed by the fact of public appearance. She remembered the time she had seen a well-known newsreader in a city centre pub. He was drinking a pint of Bass, but he did not seem to be like any other man she had ever known. The tan, the laugh, the precise part in the silver hair seemed to have been designed to perform functions that were alien to the rest of the people in the bar. He did not share the natural pallor possessed by natives of the city, the dark eyes and faces apt to suffering. Women began to comment that he was better-looking on television. The men said that he was queer. The atmosphere became more aggressive and Heather saw that his presence seemed to offer an insult to the inhabitants of the bar. She recalled that when the man left there was a sudden outpouring of relief, people buying drinks, succumbing to generous impulses. This was quickly followed by another mood. People began to feel humbled, a little sad. They avoided eye-contact with their neighbours. They began to mourn the departure of a shining emissary.

When they brought Victor in he seemed taller than she remembered. He smiled and waved at his mother, gave Heather a quick grin. He punched the air with his fist when he passed Big Ivan and Willie Lambe. These were public gestures which he performed graciously. Heather thought they were rehearsed. There was an impression of meticulous preparation. Big Ivan and Willie Lambe were sitting several rows behind Heather, wearing borrowed suits and looking like the morose elders of a rigorous congregation.

Heather had not seen him since his arrest and she felt his presence awakening the ache of sexual memory, an intricate need directed at the man with the brown skin sitting in the witness box. He was smiling, but she felt he was perplexed by the proceedings and lacked a sense of his own jeopardy.

He would arrive at the flat unexpectedly in the afternoon and they would sit on the sofa watching television for hours. Old serials, long-running family sagas. Victor would look in the *TV Times* to find out when the cartoons were on. The *Roadrunner* was his favourite. He laughed out loud at the coyote's attempts to catch the roadrunner. The cartoons were full of things he admired. Doggedness, endurance of pain, the inexplicable capacity for survival. Heather preferred old films with romantic characters. Anything that would affirm the sorrow belonging to love, its sustaining grief. She liked Victor to touch her at the end of an old film when she felt tearstained and pliant. Put his hands under her blouse, slip her underwear off beneath her skirt. When she was a teenager she discovered that you learned something from the way a man undressed you. Some went at it like a grim task but Victor did it well, without thinking about it. She had the sensation then of surrendering to a childlike feeling, tears running down her cheeks. He would say dirty words close to her ear. Cunt. The television would be on in the background, which was exciting, like people walking past not knowing what you were doing. Sex with Victor could take a long time. There were lulls, setbacks, small triumphs, but they always seemed to be moving in the same direction towards a particular and timely conclusion. Sometimes she would open her eyes and look up at him and know that she would die if he left her then.

The case did not take long. A tall thin-faced barrister announced that the Crown were withdrawing the charges. He did not mention the death of Hacksaw or the confession. Victor's brief made a speech which Heather could not hear. McClure touched her arm. He had told her several days earlier that Victor would be re-arrested and interned as soon as he left the courthouse so she had planned to wait outside, have a few quick words, touch his arm. As she left she saw that Dorcas hadn't moved. She realized that Dorcas did not know that Victor would be re-arrested. She had a smile on her face which suggested that she thought he was scot-free.

On the courthouse steps she was disappointed for Victor that there were no journalists, the roar and press of men with cameras, the snatched interview. She knew that their absence was a kind of humiliation for him. There were no confused voices, the released prisoner emerging looking winded and poorly with the photographers working towards the vital image, the prisoner's timeless stance of reprieve.

There were four detectives waiting at the door and an armoured Cortina at the bottom of the steps with its engine running. When Victor came out two of the detectives took him on the run, propelling him down the steps. Reaching around one of them she took his hand, running herself to keep up and feeling that something terrible would take place if she released him. At the bottom one of the detectives pushed her away.

'Victor.'

She watched as they pushed him into the car. The car pulled away with its doors still open. When she turned back she saw Dorcas' eyes following it. Vigilant. Lost in the bleak strategies of deception.

Long Kesh internment camp stood on a flat piece of ground to the south of the city. Approaching it you felt as if this empty land went on for ever, that this was the remote interior, sparsely inhabited, of a troubled continent. There were thin plantations of fir trees, a suggestion of wetlands, clouds massing on the horizon.

The sodium lights on the perimeter of the camp could be seen from a great distance. As you closed on it you could see barbed wire and the roofs of huts. It could have been an exploration camp or a construction village. There were the same structures, empty oil drums, areas of litter and rusting spare parts. These were the means by which these places proclaimed themselves as achievements of the century, maintained on the point of abandonment. Windswept and temporary habitations that seem the invention of the solitary mind. A makeshift acreage of the spirit.

Inside the camp was divided into cages. Barbed wire compounds surrounding Nissen huts coated with flaking green paint. You had the impression of a place left in headlong retreat, but looking closely you could see dog-handlers patrolling the perimeter and soldiers with heavy machine-guns in watch-towers. The place seemed to have been deliberately constructed along the lines of a Second World War POW camp. There was evidence of military nostalgia, a secret ache for wartime captivity, Red Cross parcels and daring escape attempts.

Each paramilitary unit had a separate cage. Provisional and official IRA, INLA, UVF, UDA. An officer in charge dealt with the prison authorities. Regular escape attempts were made but the prisoners and authorities seemed to be in agreement that these attempts should be amateurish and easily foiled.

Victor joined the UVF cage. A kind of military discipline

was enforced within each cage. The huts here were dominated by the ex-soldiers who had been lifted when internment was first introduced. They were deeply involved in questions of rank and military protocol. A man was posted permanently on the roof of each hut to receive messages from each compound. Inmates were required to stand when the OC entered the room.

Victor's OC was Arthur Glennie, whom he had known on the outside. He belonged to the old UVF, men who had harboured a grudge for so long it was part of their nature. It stretched over decades and was added to almost daily by the betrayals of government and the weaknesses of politicians and newspapers. They were suspicious of the younger men feeling that their hatred lacked depth and authority. They regarded themselves as possessing a unique rage and sought to instil a long-lived and instructive rancour. Glennie met Victor at the gate of the compound. He was a stocky man, slightly taller than Victor. He stared at him with hostility. His facial expressions lacked spontaneity as if they were carefully prepared beforehand then memorized as part of a set exercise in belligerence.

'Word has it you're a troublemaker, Kelly.'

'Wouldn't believe all you hear, Arthur.'

'Don't want none of your trouble in here.'

'I wouldn't want to wreck any cosy arrangements you got.'

'Heard tell you'd a smart mouth on you too. You might think you're the big man on the outside, son, but you're fuck-all in here. I heard about that stunt you pulled with Hacksaw McGrath in the Crumlin Road. Just to let you know, there's no freelancing in here. Everything happens in here goes through me, do you follow?'

'I'm right with you, Arthur.'

'You'd better be. Come the hard man here you'll find out what's what, so you will.'

Victor was given a bed in the hut beside the door. There was a low locker for his possessions beside the bed. Like the rest of the furniture in the hut the bed and locker were dented and chipped and the bed creaked with a forgotten sound when he lay down on it. At night the wooden floor shifted and groaned and the tin walls banged in the wind. Like a fucking refugee camp, Victor said. During the day men picked their way through the mud and gathered in groups by the wire. Two men from the same street would talk quietly together all day, exchanging accounts of people they had known or the particular way light fell across the street on November evenings. Others were aware of the comprehensive rustle of assent in these conversations and left them alone. They recognized the myth involved and the inherent virtue belonging to words of home nurtured through generations of the forlorn.

The bed next to Victor's was occupied by Ian Barnes, someone he had heard of. On the outside he was known as Biffo and he had a reputation for sudden violence. He was held in deep respect. Even his victims recognized that his savagery was impersonal. There was an elemental fury touching on a lapse of nature.

At first Victor thought that Glennie had put him beside Barnes so that he could keep an eye on him. On the first night Victor waited until lights out before he began to probe.

'Barnes.'

'What?'

'Biffo Barnes. What class of a name's that? Like something took from the fucking *Beano*.' Victor was trying to tell him he's paltry, a goon in primary colours doomed to comic failure.

Barnes didn't reply. It was too late when Victor saw his arm crossing the space between the beds, a sleepy movement that left Barnes' hand on Victor's outside the covers. The grip began to tighten, crushing his knuckles together, slowly reaching the point where pain crossed over into the unbearable. Barnes still didn't speak. He held Victor's fist as if it was an apparatus requiring inch-perfect control.

Victor could hear Barnes' quiet breathing in the dark. The voice of a sleeping man in another part of the hut lost in an avenue of memory and hurt. He felt lucid and relaxed despite the pressure on his hand. He realized that Barnes' act was not hostile and that he trusted Victor to understand that he had reached a knowledge of the nature of pain and its discreet imperatives. It was a claim to kinship. When Barnes silently removed his hand Victor realized he had an ally.

Victor and Barnes spent most of their time together following this incident. Barnes seldom spoke but he seemed content to listen to Victor, who had begun to regard the period of imprisonment as one of necessary exile. He read a book about revolutionary leaders he got from the library. Men who found themselves in a period of waiting which caused anxiety to governments. Men who waited in jungles and dingy provincial towns suffering from hardship until their thought was refined to a necessary pitch, a haunting cadence of destruction and liberation.

Victor found that when he was with Barnes the other inhabitants of the hut did not approach them. When they were together in the canteen at dinner, Victor talking and Barnes listening, the others did not speak, as if they feared the consequences of interrupting such dark parlance. The two men ignored Glennie's attempts to impose discipline on them.

'Here comes the fucking Führer.'

'Sieg Heil, Glennie.'

Winter began. The water taps froze in the morning. Bleak winds howled through the unprotected camp. The sense of isolation increased. Men gathered furtively around transistor radios. The news transmissions seemed to have acquired an underground quality, with weak signals and atmospheric static. The news was of bombs, sectarian killings and other direful events. Letters from home were suspect; the family tidings seemed inauthentic, strained, composed at gunpoint. There were several fist-fights in the shower block for which Glennie blamed Victor and Biffo. He arranged with the authorities for them to be removed unless they agreed to do lookout duty, sitting on the roof of the hut waiting for pre-arranged signals. They were given the evening shift and sat in silence, wrapped in blankets and watching the sun set like some vengeful fixture of the November sky, the landscape before them reddened with foreboding. Often they stayed up after nightfall, refusing Glennie's order to descend. Their shapes were visible from the other cages, posed on a bleak and landlocked terrain, motionless figures acquiring a permanence which seemed impervious, amoral, immune to entreaty.

part two

fourteen

Jim Curran left the snooker hall at a quarter past twelve and walked towards the Cliftonville Road. He had been playing snooker. He played every night. It was something a man could lose himself in. The green baize under hooded lights, men standing in the shadows along the wall, a purposeful drawing together, attentive to the passage and reclusive click of the balls. Curran loved the studied movements from place to place around the table, sighting along the cue and selecting their footing with precision as if they were working towards a theoretical end, an abstract perfection. Something a man could seek guidance in.

He appreciated the clarity of thought that he brought away with him when he walked home from the club. He had an exhaustive knowledge of the great sportsmen who had come from the city. People whose names you rarely saw in books. Men of icy control and self-knowledge whose greatest victories grew in his mind as feats of unendurable loneliness. Curran had a deep respect for the sporting figures of the past. Rinty Monaghan. Dixie Dean.

It seemed that he could see the city clearly on nights like this and it was a place of age and memory. He thought about the *Titanic* built in the shipyard, the closed linen mills, the derelict shirt factories, the streets of houses built for workers and other edifices constructed by speculators who seemed to have this modern city in mind, their designs weathered down to create a setting for injured lives; this city like gaunt others they had created on shallow, muddy deltas or desolate coasts guided by infallible principles of abandonment.

At first he didn't see the yellow Escort emerge from a side-street, its motor idling. He had travelled another hundred yards before he became aware of the car following him at walking pace, keeping its distance in a way that seemed obedient, as if it were awaiting a command that he might make. He did not alter his pace. It could be the police. It could be a taxi looking for an address. Nevertheless he looked along the street for shelter, a houselight, some warm billet to offset against the sudden conviction of lasting solitude. There was a row of locked garages to his right and the wall of a motorworks to his left. He could hear the noise of traffic in the distance, a sound he had been unaware of for years coming to him now as if there was something gentle-natured and sorrowing in the distance. It made him think of a country song about mothers that brought a tear to his eye. Thinking about this he stumbled on the pavement and immediately heard the car behind him rev wildly. He began to run. He thought that if he could only reach the end of the street. An image of Roger Bannister breaking the four-minute mile came into his head. A man in flapping white shorts and singlet running with his knees high and elbows tucked, upright and fleet, determined to imbue his passage with dignity, aware that history would demand no less of the moment.

He imagined that he was passing people in the street. A pair of lovers in a doorway fixed in an attitude of solace, a drunk watching him mildly, as though inclined to leniency on the basis that much of life propels men into headlong necess-ities. He felt that the dead from his past were in the shadows. Parents, brothers, uncles. He had the impression that they wore expressions of strange urging. He felt that the untiring dead were somehow gaining on him now, the soft patter of their ghostly sprints almost audible. When the car drew level with him he knew that he had lost. A man spoke to him from the passenger window.

'What's your hurry, big lad?'

Curran stopped and bent over double, gasping for breath. The car door opened and three men got out. One of them was holding a tyre iron.

'You're coming with us, son.'

'A big trip in the motor car.'

'Fuck's sake mister you're not fit at all. Wee run like that and you can't get a breath.'

'He'll be fit by the time we get done with him, Victor.'

'Fit for fuck-all.'

Curran held up one hand. He wanted permission to catch his breath before speaking, a respite so that he could begin to form words again. Please.

Ryan's father died in December. His mother rang him early in the morning. Your father died during the night, she said. Her voice was weary. It was just another thing her husband had done to alarm her. It was news of an affair. It was sitting at the kitchen table with him while he explained the reasons why they had no money. He had spoken her name just once in the middle of the night using the same tone of long-held grievance which he had used to describe the other disasters in his life. She had left the bed and started a series of calm phone calls. Her response to his death was scripted in the same rich language of irreparable fault which she had used during his lifetime.

As Ryan was packing to travel home the phone rang again. It was Margaret.

'Your mother rang me,' she said, 'I'm sorry.' Ryan wasn't surprised. He knew that Margaret and his mother had become closer since they had separated. He tried to imagine them speaking on the phone to each other, both adept at extracting the marginal satisfactions to be had from disappointment in love.

'How do you feel?'

'I don't know. I wished he was dead so often.'

'That's different.'

It was always one of the subjects they could talk about. Ryan and his father. Margaret defending him. Ryan bitterly identifying with his weaknesses. What had most offended him in the end was the half-hearted way his father had gone about deception, the offhand duplicity. The lies he told were borrowed, makeshift. Ryan and his mother always knew when he wasn't telling the truth. He took on an unconvincing, dispirited expression. A rained-on and hopeless look. His arguments possessed a commanding lack of conviction, delivered in an imperious whine that left them feeling helpless.

'I feel like he's got away with something. I don't believe him. He's my da. He shouldn't have died like that in that well I just did it way of his. I feel like I'm owed some sort of explanation somewhere. I could have forgiven him if he'd died heroically. Called for me at the last moment so he could hold my hand and look up at me so's I could graciously forgive him.'

'Swelling violins, fade to weeping women outside bedroom door. Wise up, Ryan.'

It was what he needed. A voice to cut through the rudimentary panic he felt at his father's death. The feeling of being lost in transit somewhere in a neglected landscape with the likelihood of dark weather ahead.

'It's not anybody's fault,' Margaret said softly. 'I'll see you down there.'

He felt the effort she was making to inject the extra note of gracious summary and took it for heartfelt, whispering her name down the line before she hung up.

It was evening before he left, passing the red-brick semi-detached suburbs on the outskirts of the city that he had once watched from the bus on day-trips as a child, with a feeling that there was something deep-set and mysterious about these houses, a suggestion that part of life at least could be bought. He imagined coming home at night and going under the deep shade of the laburnum at the gate, putting out his fingers to the glass handle of a porch door, being greeted by a mother who approached him with low-keyed and costly cries of love.

The traffic died five miles out of the town. He passed through a succession of small towns. There was sectarian graffiti on the walls, policemen carrying old-fashioned Mausers with wooden stocks and looking like a poorly armed Balkan militia, dull and enduring. Dour churches on the outskirts, shops closed at five, a sense of the future indefinitely postponed.

Then the empty caravan parks on the long stretch outside the town. Sand blowing in from the dunes, pitted aluminium, yellow gas cylinders. It looked like a place for the shiftless, the desperate. He thought of it during the summer. Bare-armed women setting meals on collapsible picnic tables. They looked alert and temperate, putting out paper cups with care and a sense that this was as much as they were permitted, these impaired habitations on the edge of the disconsolate. It was the women who gathered and talked quietly outside the shower-block in the morning as though it was a terminus for the unwary. And it was the women who lay awake at night listening to sand hissing in the caravan chassis and to children making sounds in their sleep to complement that sound, so that they felt a parent's faint dread at their children's access to the windblown and strange.

The esplanade was deserted. The arcades were closed for the winter, cloud gathering out at sea. The front seemed like a location designed for an off-season drama, carefully lit to suggest dereliction and small but ominous happenings.

There were cars lined on either side of the pavement outside the council house. Ryan walked in past strangers, who took his hand or touched his shoulder as he passed. He was aware he was being studied, people giving him their attention as a grave, courteous bounty. The only son. Letting him know that this was no small matter. He hugged his mother without speaking to her and went over to the open coffin. Beneath the waxy glow the plain expectant face. An expression of readiness that seemed to have been laboured over, worked at in the long sinking away from the light. He was shaken by the dead man's air of preparation, the honest facing of death's calm interrogative.

When he raised his head he saw Margaret at the other side of the room. She was looking at him, it seemed, with her breath held as if the face he had lifted to her would disintegrate on exposure to air. He saw that she had lost the weight that she had put on during their six years of marriage – putting it on as a form of protest, he thought at the time. Abandoning that which he was supposed to love in her and withdrawing into a meagre guile, determined to be unworthy.

Later he went outside for air. He leaned against a car smoking a cigarette. It was a still night. The cars gleaming in the dark, reflecting a fragmentary light. The roofs of the houses opposite profiled against the sky. He saw the front door open and Margaret coming down the path. He waited for her to reach him.

'Hello.'

'Hello yourself. What are you doing out here?'

'Nothing sinister. Getting air. Did my mother send you?'

'Shit Ryan, don't talk like that. That sly stuff. Your mother's in there with the aunts. She can't stand their guts. They're wandering around dabbing at the eyes with tissues. Your ma says they're Protestants. Says they've got big margarine faces.'

'How's the job?' She was teaching at a technical college in the city.

'You hear yourself droning. You can't help seeing yourself the way they see you.'

'What way's that?'

'I don't know, frantic, living on some scary edge. They keep pushing. The hell with that though. How's life on the front line? The daring investigative reporter.'

'Strange I suppose. It's like me and Coppinger got all tied up in these knife killings. He'll be lining up suspects in the bar of the Four-in-Hand next. It scares the shit out of me. I want to grow old and report on the Lord Mayor's show.'

'Mouse. How is the greasy old bastard anyhow?'

'Greasy as ever. Seriously though he seems to be getting deeper and deeper in. I hardly ever see him. He's like a character out of a book, knows fate's out to get him.'

'Tell him to be careful from me. You too.' He felt the return of a familiar anger at her reply. The perfunctory tone. He wanted to feel that she was still suffering the loss of him.

'Want to go for a drink?' he asked.

'At your father's funeral?'

'All the more reason.'

'I don't think so. I think I can tell what would happen.'

'Nothing would happen. We'd have a drink is all.'

'Everything would happen. It'd all happen. I think I'm going back to the house. You should too.'

'I'll go in when I'm ready to go in. This is my show.'

'Suit yourself.'

He watched her walk away from him, taking with her the momentary reassurance he had felt, an edifying fury which faded as she left, drawing it after her into the darkness.

He could not remember much about the funeral. A sense that it had been recovered from archives. The documented past painfully reconstructed and enacted to purge a troubling historical remainder. Men with weathered faces, farmers from the mountain hinterland, gathered at points along the route. Scenes of rehearsed grief. The brown coffin's weight and awkward shapes; the resisting bulk designed to stress that death is a difficult terrain to enter.

There was rain as well. Squally cold showers that seemed to occur at crucial moments. Walking from the car to the church, darkening the sky as they stood at the graveside and carrying the priest's voice away into a lost and ruinous place. People coughed and reached for handkerchiefs and exchanged glances which enquired as to how they had found themselves here in the worst of all possible places.

When it was over he walked towards the car park with his mother, holding her by the elbow. Her walk was calm and dignified. She had not cried during the funeral, which surprised him. He wondered what way she had decided to frame her mourning and realized that she had decided to defer to the death as though it was a doctor or a solicitor or other tactful and convincing professional. As he was unlocking the car Margaret approached them. She kissed his mother, gave her a solicitous look. His mother put her hand on Margaret's forearm. These were events which did not include him. He felt their approval of each other. He felt the weight of future exchanges. Phone calls. Shopping trips. He remembered how during their marriage Margaret would swap clothes with his mother and how they would engage in small financial trans-actions with repayments scrupulously adhered to. It repre-sented a tautness in their relationship. No detail was too small. The world was full of unexpected traps and the smallest event had scope for disaster. This was handed on from mother to daughter: to be adequate to the small tasks at hand, to be serious, to make store against loss.

The two women talked in low voices. Come for the week-end. Ring me if you feel. Tones of urgent arrangement before they turned to the man standing at the driver's door as though he was a task to be shared between them, a shoddy thing to be held and turned against a revealing light.

'Listen,' Margaret said to him, 'give me a ring when you get back.' Her words included his mother so that Ryan didn't know whether he was supposed to ring or whether Margaret was speaking in deference to the older woman. Either way it was an opening, a reward held out for endeavour. As Ryan watched her return to her own car he felt the revival of an old lust, strongest when she wore formal dress. The black patent high heels, the long skirt in strict pleats, the tension in her calves under black tights made her look tailored into a sexual geometry, a close-fitting garment of the heart.

Ryan stayed for a few days after the funeral. His mother seemed barely aware of his presence. Occasionally he found her looking at him with an expression of mild regret.

She had made no attempt to remove his father's belongings. His jacket behind the door, the worn shaving brush with dried foam in the bristles, the drawers of clothing. Ryan thought they looked indecent. He thought about personal belongings scattered across open fields after an air crash; an intimate debris, deprived of context, looking hapless and betrayed.

He spent the days walking in the town. The arcades were empty. People walked dogs on the beach when the tide was out. He waited for the feeling that he used to get in winter. The sense of off-season grace; an elaborate nostalgia created by empty cafés and car tyres in the rain and the town's vulnerable infinites of deserted car parks, early darkness.

That Friday night he went down to the Harbour bar, coming in off the street at seven o'clock with rain in his hair. There were only a few men wearing working clothes in the bar. There was a pool table and a poker machine. The television was on with the volume down and he watched it as he waited for the barman. He noticed that one of the men at the end of the bar was staring at him.

He ordered a hot whiskey. He enjoyed being in a bar in the space between the day and the night-time crowd. There was an agreed lull – a grant to the restless and unconvinced.

The man who had been staring at him came over. He was wearing blue overalls and labourer's boots caked in red clay. His face was streaked in building-site dirt and his eyes were so bloodshot it was difficult to detect any white in them. He looked like a model for a lurching, unwieldy rage of earth. He stood in front of Ryan swaying, his fists hanging by his sides.

'Fuck are you looking at?' he said suddenly. Ryan realized that this wasn't political or sectarian. This was not one of the poised and subtle forms of violence he examined for its redemptive qualities. This was an unforeseen primal anger.

'Said what the fuck are you looking at?' the man repeated. Ryan didn't reply. He felt remote as if he had already taken the blow and accepted an obscure guilt.

'I don't know what he's looking at but it's looking back at him anyhow. Leave him be Raymie. Get on away out of the road and give the man peace.'

The man blinked, his eye switching to the speaker behind Ryan's shoulder. He shrugged and walked away. Ryan turned towards the woman's voice. She was vaguely familiar behind the make-up on her round face. The blusher, eye-shadow, lipstick laid on with a heavy hand as though she had earned the right to wear this gaudy face, building it up in the mirror with astute touches until she found herself staring at a knowing and vigilant accessory.

'I thought I was headed for casualty,' Ryan said.

'State he was in he'd of probably fell on his arse lifting his fist. Still and all, it took the woman's touch.' Her laugh had an ashen sound which Ryan hadn't expected.

'Could I get you a drink?'

'I'll get my own. Still and all I'll pull up a stool here. I don't think I'll get much chat out of them others.'

She sat on the stool beside him and ordered a Bacardi and coke. She had a big body which moved easily under a loose blouse, as if it was accustomed to addressing itself to physical certitudes.

'Still,' he said, 'you handled him well.'

'That class of a man's easy. Wee buns. Goes home loaded, wife doesn't talk to him for a week, giving him the old picture but no sound. Inside a day he's eating the face off himself saying sorry and starting to hate her guts. Next thing he's off on the drink again. Doesn't know who he feels worse about.'

'That's pretty harsh.'

'Pretty true.' He noticed that the black eye-liner on her bottom lids gave her the look of a shy nocturnal mammal surprised in headlights, and he remembered where he had seen her before.

'The Ambassador,' he said.

'What?'

'The Ambassador cinema. I used to see you there, Friday, Saturday nights.'

'I don't get you.'

'You're from the town. You used to go to the Ambassador, sit up in the balcony with a crowd. You'd be tossing lit cigarettes into the stalls and all.'

'Maybe. It's a long time ago.'

It seemed that way to Ryan as well but he remembered her as an amateur version of the person beside him, the glow of a cigarette in the back row of the balcony, a girl's laughter out of the darkness. There was little else. A few names, half-seen faces, fragments of voices carried towards him on a dark portage of recollection.

'What's your name?'

'Ryan.'

'I know now. Your da.'

'Aye.'

'I was sorry to hear. He used to teach us swimming down at the baths. We never used to talk all that much. I remember it would of froze the bum off you down there.'

He could see the pool tiling, the rusting iron grilles and dank pipes that filled the pool when the tide was in. He could see the weed-covered handrails, the whole thing like a raised hulk, green and dripping, a sense of horror about it as though ghastly corpses still floated in submerged companionways.

'One of many jobs he couldn't hold on to.'

'You shouldn't speak ill of the dead.'

Margaret had said something similar to him. He resented the incursions upon his father's death. It was a place which now belonged to him; a location in a border country, subject to eerie winds, scant rainfall.

'I'm sorry,' she said. 'My big mouth.'

'That's all right.'

'Were you close?'

'I tried to avoid his mistakes.'

'Did you?'

'I found a whole set of new ones.'

He felt that this was what he needed. Conversation with a strange woman in a bar. Laconic words. Someone to admire him for having survived his father, for having wrestled all that age and weariness and spite from his grasp.

He ordered another drink in the spirit of winter evenings in seaside bars, salt spray blowing against the windows with a frugal, corrosive sound.

Afterwards he tried to piece it together. The small dance floor, the music. The bar had gradually filled up without their noticing. Lying back in bed he tried to recall a sequence of events. His head ached. The bedroom stank with the toxic remnant of alcohol. She had said that she was living in the city now. He thought back to the disco, the other dancers with their faces set and exultant. She had mentioned a man. He searched his memory feeling like a dazed survivor wandering in the smouldering wreckage. Holding her above the hips, the material of her dress slipping against the skin, the indentations of her underwear then, the hard and elementary patterns. An old joke he'd made with girls when he was seventeen, leading her into it:

'Do you fuck?'

'Yes, do you?'

'Yes.'

'Then fuck off.'

She had to stop dancing to laugh at this. He moved her towards the exit before she had recovered, forcing her through the crowd in front of them, people stepping out of the way and looking at him strangely as though he had just made a peremptory arrest.

Outside in the car park rain glistening on parked cars, dark, wet tarmac, an unforgiving light between zones of shadow, He pushed her back among the stacked beer kegs and empty crates. It was a setting for small lusts, assignations of guilt and consequence. She was still laughing. He put his hands under her blouse. He had never been with this type of woman before. He touched her breasts, the reposed and forceful weight. He thought of Margaret whose body seemed suddenly scaled down into a model of unnecessary refinement. She had stopped laughing then and begun to respond to his kiss. He felt her begin to take control. When he opened his eyes she was looking at him thoughtfully.

The phone began to ring downstairs and he waited for his mother to answer it. When the ring continued he realized that she must have gone out and pulled on a pair of trousers.

'Ryan?' It was Coppinger. His voice had an echoing quality on the phone as though he was standing in a large, frigid space.

'We've got another knife job. I told you it was going to happen.'

'Congratulations.'

'James Frances Curran, age forty-seven, last seen coming from a snooker hall and headed for the Cliftonville Road. Found after an anonymous phone call. Police have refused to comment but locals say his throat was cut and the body placed in a kneeling position with the head tilted back. I hung around the Royal last night. Seems a very sharp instrument was used. A hunting knife was suggested.'

'It's all there isn't it.'

'Official silence, the body posed. All we can get is cause of death to be established.'

'It's understandable. People would be panicking.'

'Shite. The whole city knows about it anyhow. Do you know what they're calling them? The Resurrection Men.'

'Like the grave robbers?'

'Aye. Wouldn't be surprised if they were putting it about themselves. Droll lads so they are.'

Ryan's mind was crowded with images of horror. His father had told him about the Resurrection Men. Operating out of cheap wharfside boarding houses, smothering the drunk and elderly with pillows and shipping the bodies to medical schools in Edinburgh, their veins pumped full of chemicals from a brass syringe, an abiding stink like a sharp taste in the mouth. These are the lungs, this is the heart. Mothers dead in childbirth, paupers, foundlings, travellers in the uneventful dark, their faces fixed in a loose, formaldehyde gape.

'It suits them. My head's away this morning. Tell me what it means.'

'I'll talk to you when you get back. You any plans?'

'I'm leaving this evening. By the way, Margaret was asking for you.'

'Was she?'

'She said how is the greasy old bastard.' The three of them used to go drinking together. Margaret drunk would argue politics with Coppinger. Fifty years of Protestant rule, housing rights, employment rights. A dominion of the righteous. He would listen to her without comment. Sometimes Ryan thought he encouraged it. It seemed to confirm worries he had about himself. Coppinger had never told Ryan anything about his background except that he had come to the city from the country. Somewhere Ryan had gained an impression of make-shift congregational halls, the just gathering from outlying farms in the darkness, sparse and godfearing. Margaret understood this better than Ryan. The bare, scrubbed places in the soul; work from dawn to dusk, Sabbath observance, the wrath of the righteous.

'Is she gone back to the city?'

'Straight after the funeral.'

'I might give her a ring. She's a good girl, so she is.'

Ryan knew the way that Coppinger regarded her. It was a kind of flattery. It made her see herself baking bread, collecting children from school. A dream of well-regarded and admirable motherhood. Honest, not beautiful, plainspoken. The ancestral pain of love.

'I'll see you tonight in the York,' he told Coppinger, before hanging up.

He replaced the receiver feeling lost. Upstairs he went through his pockets before dressing, searching through the debris of coins, wadded tissues, broken cigarettes. How many times had he stood attempting to reconstruct the events of an evening from these fragments? He thought of dimly lit artifacts, difficult, allusive objects. Among them he came across a damp cigarette packet with her address on it. He had walked her part of the way home. After the car park they were both happy to revert to people who had been brought up in the town. They talked about first kisses, café jukeboxes, small episodes fixed in the resonant dismay of adulthood. They held hands and walked along the esplanade. He asked her if he would see her again. She said no, that her man had just come back from a journey. He asked for her address and she had written it on the cigarette packet. When they reached the end she hailed a taxi and rode away without looking round. As he got into the car to drive back to the city Ryan felt the mood of the night before still with him. His mother did not come to the door to wave him off. A sea mist hung over the town. People drifting apart, his mother in her armchair, a woman's white blouse in the back of a taxi. The air was soft and moist. People and buildings faded into it, features perceived vaguely, as if the town was temporary, constructed in the vague materials of leave-taking and return.

fifteen

Willie Lambe had bought the knives when he had hopes of working at the fish plant, joining the men who worked for piece rates on the filleting line. He had seen them once, the knives moving at such speed through the fishes that their flesh twitched as though granted unendurable life.

Shortly after Victor's release Willie had set a brown paper parcel on the bar at the Pot Luck and unwrapped it to reveal the knives. The bar fell silent as Victor picked them up and handled them. Sheffield Stainless. Go through you like you weren't there. A rapture of design. He put the knife down on the bar beside the other two, soft light falling on them through the window, so that they looked like something inscribed on the counter, a word or versatile phrase of extinction.

They had used Willie's car for the Curran job. Afterwards he had spent most of the night cleaning blood from the seats. The next morning he took his mother out, watching her in the mirror in case she detected vestiges of mortality underlying the smell of Jeyes fluid. She asked him about the smell and he said that Big Ivan was drunk and got sick in the back. Every time he thought of what had happened he squeezed his thighs together. Biffo hitting your man a dig with the hatchet every now and then, Victor sitting quietly in the front seat, every so often telling Biffo to take it easy, not to be too hard on him, like a concerned citizen. As they got closer to the spot Victor got that look on him, his eyes half-shut like he was trying to remember something, telling Willie which way to go. Turn right. Left at the lights. Snapping it out. All the time looking to check your man on the back seat.

He told Willie to stop the motor and turn off the engine. Your man was still conscious, Willie noticed. Half his head beat in and he was sat there in the back dead calm like he's won first fucking prize, a trip to Glencairn gardens with the Nolan sisters depart 8.00 a.m. sharp. Big Ivan gets out with the hatchet and does this hop skip around the car like a Red Indian waving the hatchet and busting a rib to himself. Rain dance. Biffo lifts this Taig out of the car dead gentle, Big Ivan still laughing fit to bust. It would of froze you in that alley. Biffo puts your man kneeling on the ground then stands back. There still isn't a peep out of your man. Victor come over until he was standing beside him with Big Ivan still leaping around clean mad and there's blood everywhere in the alley. It was the first time ever Willie ever thought about the length of a second. Biffo with that big long face on him hanging down to the ground. Victor saying 'knife' to him like it was 'scalpel' in an operation, and your man on the ground watching the whole go, not saying nothing. Driving away with Big Ivan talking about how your man would stiff up dead quick because of the cold in the alley.

It was around then that Victor started to see the first graffiti appearing in the derelict Catholic streets that had been burnt out before the army were sent in. The television had shown the occupants camped at the border fifty miles away, living in tents. The parents in food queues advancing shabbily. He was impressed by the graffiti. It was a rumour of approval in the narrow streets. Resurrection Men 1. Taigs 0. It confirmed that he was on the right track. It was the first sign of a legend taking shape, a dark freight in the soul of the city. He believed he understood the silence of the media, the massive reserve they brought to the details of the Curran job and the others which had gone before. He understood a painful inching towards the truth.

When he was released after a year in Crumlin Road and Long Kesh he spent the first week driving around the city absorbing change. Security gates were placed around the badly bombed city centre and they were closed each night as though to protect an exalted ruin of commerce. During that week he drove several times to the docks in the evening. A lot of the housing and port buildings had been demolished. He closed his eyes and recalled with difficulty street after street peopled through the wavering salvage of memory; characters closed in their incomplete histories.

The Zephyr he had once sat in was gone from the quay. He went to stand at the water's edge in virtual darkness, the sea moving gently beneath him; a sense of containment in the dock. No wild nights here, the isobars packed and bad weather static on the sea area forecast. Out in the empty channel he could see the red and green marker buoys flashing although there was nothing for them to guide. He thought about the Zephyr, John Dillinger and the Wife of the Month. They were what he needed now, especially Dillinger and his steadfast unwillingness to resign himself to the flawed verities of his life. But all he felt was the first chill of mortality in the place where, in prison, he had dreamed he would find himself alone with his thoughts and confirmed invincible.

Heather waited for a week after her return before he came to see her. As soon as she saw him she knew he had been with another woman in the meantime, some thin Shankill girl with hipbones you could hang your hat on who found her life stranded in a desperate interim. The knowledge didn't bother Heather and Victor was anything but apologetic. When she opened the door he walked in without looking at her. She followed him into the living room. He watched her as if she was liable to edge out of sight. She stared quietly back working out what the last year had done to him. Living here she had got used to men coming out of prison or internment. To the young men it was a coming into manhood, their bounty in the world. It was different for the older men. At first they were softly spoken, careful in their movements. Later there were drunken rages and accusations of adultery. They regarded their friends with suspicion. It was as if the existence they had left had been replaced by a subtly changed counterfeit.

Victor showed no sign of either but he had changed. She had to search in her own past to find anything approaching the way she saw him now. Her family had belonged to a small Baptist church down a side street near the promenade. The women frowned on make-up. They wore hats and carried small patent handbags as though these were the credentials of a careful belief. The plain inside of the church seemed worked down to the bare structure. The men wore black suits. They wanted God to see them as attached and dependable. It had been strange therefore to file in one Sunday morning to see a different minister in the pulpit. He was younger than the usual man, with a pocked face and hair combed back. He gripped the wooden edge as though it was a struggle with satanic powers just to be standing there. His face spoke of remorse-less struggle. When he spoke to say that their minister was ill and unable to attend his voice was ravaged and wintry. After the ceremony no one mentioned him and he had never returned.

It was this quality she saw in Victor, the way he looked at her flat like it was a wilderness, a wind-blasted place. She had heard about people who had converted in prison, turned good-living. She thought there was a trace of mystic zeal in his eyes.

Later in bed however it was the same as it had always been. A largesse that they laboured over, watchful and dili-gent, striving towards the silence afterwards. It was not until they lay together in a memorial calm that she felt the change again. The vestiges of solitude, she thought. The compelling remnants of night after night spent alone in a cell.

In the following weeks he began to spend much more time with McClure, which worried her. McClure had taken over a lock-up shop and was renting bootleg super eight films. Westerns, detective stories, horror films, murder mysteries. He kept a stock of pornographic films under the counter which he would show in the Pot Luck after closing time. McClure liked these grainy fictions. The clothing was always old-fashioned so that the characters looked mislaid in a sexual chronology. The poorly dubbed soundtrack gave the fake moans and gasps a glacial edge. There were halting preliminaries, clumsy seductions. The voices had an edge of supplication to them.

McClure liked to watch the audience's reaction. The way that the men took on a cheated look which bespoke violence yet to come. They had expected to feel more than a doomed erotic nostalgia, an amateur sorrow that was too close for comfort.

Victor paid no attention to the film, or to the swelling anger in the audience. Instead he scanned their faces with a puzzled look as if there were a missing element. Long, yellow breasts offered in consolation.

McClure wondered what Victor would make of a film he had shot himself in a rented house in Lisburn three months before Victor was released. It featured Heather with a local building contractor, the man's body on top of her in a pose of dreadful resuscitation. Heather's eyes looked at the ceiling and it was obvious that her mind had gone blank with Valium slippage. Afterwards McClure had put five hundred pounds in her handbag. It was a fair trade for a share in the building sites the man owned in the satellite towns on that side of the city where houses were going up with such speed they seemed instantaneous.

After these showings Victor and McClure would withdraw

into a back room. The others accepted this. Big Ivan thought of an underground room in a wartime film with scattered maps with grim-faced Victor plotting campaigns with hairs-breadth precision. Willie Lambe had a frightening image of the two men in a flickering light, chill and unmoving, with etched faces, vigil kept against unremitting night. Biffo, who had joined the unit after he had been released, sat alone at the bar and kept his own dark observance.

In the storeroom McClure would take a mirror advertising Daly's Irish whiskey from the wall and set it on the table. He emptied a gram of amphetamine sulphate on to it and took a razor-blade from his pocket. He chopped the powder to make it fine and showed Victor how to roll a note. He talked in a low, instructive tone. Chop it up dead fine, that way it doesn't hurt your nose. He took pains to explain each step. A warm feeling between himself and Victor was important. A sense that this was a patient methodology coming intact through generations. Something perhaps that a father could offer to a son. A patient craft to offset against puzzlement and rage.

Must have rid a Taig.

McClure combed the white powder into two narrow lines and leaned over one with the rolled-up note held close to his face. He moved carefully up the line, erasing it from the glass. He handed the note to Victor who bowed his head to within two inches of the mirror.

'Don't breathe out,' McClure said softly. The powder was intensely white, ephemeral. Shutting his eyes Victor felt the bitter medicinal sting high up in his nose and almost immediately afterwards a chemical smart in the back of his throat.

Within ten minutes Victor was talking as he had never talked before. Language as a frantic gesturing as if each was somehow out of earshot and trying to warn the other of imminent danger. McClure's face was pushed up against Victor's, the pupils of his eyes minute. A stream of words with high-altitude clarity. A bright vocal madness. McClure pitched it towards a fluent hatred of Catholics. Their IRA. Their lucklessness. Their affectation to suffering. Their unemployment statistics. Their women's lovely offered breasts. The smallness of their needs. Their innumerable children. The commonplace of their dying.

At eight o'clock that morning McClure turned on the radio, turning the dial wildly until he got the BBC World Service news. The newscaster's voice was crisp and authoritative. He knew that his voice was being carried into the corners of the world. Each sentence was pronounced as if it were an edict to be imposed upon an unruly native population. McClure held up his hand for silence.

'The Provisional IRA has claimed responsibility for an attack on a Protestant-owned filling station on the outskirts of the city. Two men were killed and three others wounded.'

'What'd I tell you? What'd I tell you? Bastards trying to wipe us out. Cunts. We got to do a job. We got to do one on them today.' McClure nodded. Daylight coming through the small storeroom window. It was a gaunt structured moment, dense with considerations of reprisal. McClure spoke first.

'The Shamrock bar.'

'Quick drive. See a checkpoint a mile away.'

'Fast getaway.'

'Lift a taxi. Willie driving.'

'Sitting back here drinking before the fuckers know they're dead.'

'What shooting, officer? I was sat here all night.'

'Bang, bang.'

'Bang, fucking bang.'

By 12 a.m. other units in the area had been in touch. There was talk of a joint operation but Victor had the team picked. Big Ivan to hijack a taxi and act as back-up. Willie to drive. Biffo and Victor to do the job. McClure left and returned with two snub-nosed Mausers. Biffo had his own .22 pistol. Victor had the .9mm. The preparations continued all afternoon. Big Ivan cut eye- and mouth-holes in four yellow linen money-bags left over from a post office job the previous year. Men came in and offered ammunition. Other attacks were described. The weapons were handed around, weighed in the palm, discussed in terms of range and accuracy. Plain objects with an oily film. Big Ivan and Willie sat apart wearing shy grins. They were patted on the shoulder and spoken to in soft caressing voices. Their attitude suggested humility. They were prepared for a common ordeal. The other people in the bar seemed astonished to have these men among them. Talking, smiling. Men travelling in their own documented present, at ease with themselves. As heroes they were capable of larger emotions. They belonged more forcefully to the world.

Victor paced the small stage at the back of the bar. The amphetamine had removed his appetite and desire for sleep. Men coming in looked at his bloodless and drawn face with approval. It seemed like a product of lifetime abstinence. There was a selfless, driven quality of leadership. They could see fierce pieties in his eyes and those that got close to him swore to a sour, monastic odour.

At 9.36 p.m. Willie stopped the hijacked taxi outside the Shamrock bar and they all put the moneybags over their heads. Biffo and Victor got out and walked towards the doorway of the bar. The yellow moneybags made them look like the ungainly members of a rural secret society given to oath-taking.

There were about fifteen people drinking in the downstairs bar. They fell silent as the two men entered. They could see the guns in their hands and the two snub-noses stuck in their belts. There was a moment of uncertainty. The people in the bar feeling that something was expected of them, that they should shape a response out of the sudden onset of consternation. They exchanged glances, raised their eyebrows then turned to look at the men as if they had decided on a mood of apprehension. One of the men waved his gun vaguely in the direction of the drinkers.

'Prods on one end of the bar, Taigs on the other.'

Half of the people rose immediately and began to move towards the bar. They seemed grateful for the guidance offered. They went calmly to their respective ends of the bar and stood there awaiting further instructions. The rest of the people in the bar were more alert, their faces working soundlessly as they attempted to decide whether the gunmen were Catholic or Protestant, trying to come to a decision as to which end of the bar to go to. They began to mill around in the centre of the floor, knocking against each other and swearing softly. One of them, a man wearing plumber's overalls, ran into one of the hooded men. He lifted his hands and shrugged his shoulders, his face mute and beseeching. He knew what was going to happen to him and felt it necessary to enter a plea to the nearest source of omnipotence. Missed opportunities, middle-aged loss of courage, all his small spectral failings had to be taken into account. He seemed to be saying that forgiveness was difficult but not impossible and should be given priority in an atmosphere of last things. The hooded man raised his pistol and with every appearance of generosity shot him in the mouth.

The two men began to fire at random. The drinkers ran towards exits, disappeared into the toilets, lay down on the floor, stood and covered their ears. Even in a confined space the firing did not sound like shots, did not fit into the perceived idea of gunfire — the roar, the muzzle flash, the profound and vital noise that hangs in the air. The aimed shot, the squeezed trigger. A whole glamorous ethic was missing from this scene with masked men pointing guns that made a flat, non-lethal sound.

Nevertheless people were dying. The barman was on the floor, hit twice in the chest. Two men were dying in the toilets. Another lay near the door in a pool of femoral blood. The upstairs barman was shot in the stomach from the bottom of the stairs. He clasped his hands over the wound and stood like that for a long time. There was a gentle expression on his face. He wished to be considerate in his dying. The two gunmen watched in appreciation as he started to fall, tumbling down the stairs in a graceful, cinematic manner.

The two men backed out of the bar, firing as they went. They stood in the doorway, reluctant now to leave. They shot at light bulbs, mirrors, bottles behind the bar. A sound of half-hearted skirmish, fading away.

Finally they were gone. There was a smell of gunsmoke in the air, a cordite hum. There was a growing background noise from the survivors. A thin wail as they got to grips with the idea of massacre and the reek of death. A wounded man crawled across the floor until he was under a table. He needed sanctuary, somewhere he could be alone with his pain, to turn it over in his mind and begin to learn its properties. There was moaning coming from the toilets, beer dripping from an opened tap, bloody handprints on the flock wallpaper.

McClure said he hoped they hadn't left it too late for the last news. The four team members had walked into the bar with their weapons held high and their hair plastered down with sweat. They were crowded at the door and there was a movement to hoist them shoulder-high. They were like heroes from a film with John Wayne, McClure told Victor afterwards. Men in streaming yellow oilskins and exhausted expressions who have saved their community from an insane natural force of flood or landslide. There were more women than usual present. Wives and girlfriends sat at low tables in the carpeted section of the bar dressed in their best clothes.

At 11.40 McClure turned on the television above the bar. Men stood up holding their drinks. A tense silence descended. McClure located the volume button and turned to look at the audience. They held their glasses in joined hands and their solemn faces seemed lit from underneath. McClure considered their grave silence an act of devotion. The Shamrock bar was the first item on the news. The newcaster went to live pictures of the scene, the camera aimed from behind yellow incident tape. Dark figures moved in the distance across a bare tract of wet tarmac. Grey police Land-Rovers were parked diagonally under street-lights. Policemen and soldiers stood with their backs to the camera so that they could not be identified. There was an atmosphere of disinterment, grim cloaked figures working by lamplight, poisonous graveyard vapours.

When the broadcast ended Heather noticed that Victor was missing. She found him in the storeroom with the mirror and razor-blade sitting on his lap. He looked at her as if he did not remember her. She felt the dread that the elderly sometimes aroused in her. He looked like an old man, a parched wanderer in the intricate landscapes of memory.

sixteen

It was a time of anxious thought for Dorcas when Victor was
released. It would not justify her to say that he had changed
but there was a quietness in him to put her in mind of his
father James and a new badness to his temper as well. It was
also her lot to have the remarks of women in the street asking
about him all sweetness and light, but she knew a cut about a
son being in prison when she heard one. She wouldn't let them
see her mortified but smiled back saying in her heart at the
same time put the knife back in the drawer, Miss Sharp.

Sometimes she would hear noises outside the house at
night and she would be took with a fear like a seizure. The
news was a sad complaint of people shot at place of work or
blew up with bombs. There was a denial of government
protection concerning the Protestant people and the IRA had
their guns turned on the defenceless. There was no point in
turning to James for comfort as the few words he did speak
were worse than no words at all.

If Victor was involved in the protection of Protestants she
asked no questions but sometimes there was a pain like an
accusation from worry. There was an end to the visits when he
would sit at the kitchen table making you laugh fit to burst,
acting the big gangster from the pictures. He was so quiet the
first time he got out she asked was it something they done to
him in prison, because once they got you to Castlereagh or
Gough barracks they could break you like a twig, no questions
asked. It was known that the police did not hinder themselves

when it come to manhandling. When Victor was inside she wrote several times to her MP and also the chief constable but received no reply from those quarters. They made a big show of marching at funerals and putting on the big sad face on television but it was all personal ambition as far as they were concerned.

She asked Victor if he was still running with that girl Heather as she had interesting things to report as to who she was seen with while he languished. When he said sometimes, she decided however that it was a case of best say nothing. Even though it was plain to anyone with an eye in their head that the girl was used goods. But to be a mother is to know the value of silence.

It was about this time that James started to read to her from the papers about the people who were found cut with knives. He did it to deliver a shock to her. He would add detail of his own to put the heart out of you. He would be sat up in the chair by the fire and would start reading out of the blue in a voice like the voice of a minister in church that says no matter how much you fear you do not fear enough. It drove her to distraction. When he was finished he would look up at her with a glare on his face which said are you happy now?

Forbye all that he was a man and did not cease to come to her bed. For a woman and a mother the flesh is a matter of endurance. It is always women you see in the doctor's surgery. It was not as if he come with flowers. That was put aside like any worn thing after marriage. It was a matter of pride with her to maintain her figure not for his benefit. A husband is a thing like a knife. He is a cause of pain. If he was not so quiet and strange she would have said to him straight out. Go you back to your own bed. She would have said a man of your age. He was honestly like a thief or a burglar to put the fear of God into you. And other women have envious thoughts of such a quiet husband. If they knew the way he made you feel like you were due a punishment. Afterwards she would lie awake and listen to the rain and the wind like a story of their love. But she understood now the way life went that love did not enter into it as it used to, but men must punish you for their lives; and she wondered was it ever any different, even when they were just married and the baby was there and it was a case of yes but be quiet and do not wake the baby.

In the month following the Shamrock bar massacre there were two more knife murders, the victims picked up in Catholic areas and dumped nearby. Medical reports showed that the wounding was more extensive. There was evidence of frenzy, repeated slashing. It suggested that the rudiments of control had been lost.

The murders were reported in the papers but the detail was still suppressed. People examined street maps to trace possible routes used by the killers. The victims' last movements were discussed exhaustively as if this might reveal what marked you out for this kind of death. Their final moments seemed to contain something that the city needed. There might have been concealed passages of grace and people wished to secure accounts of them.

Bombings and incendiary attacks had become less frequent in the city. There was a tightening of security: parking control zones were introduced, body searches, more troops on the streets. But there had been a rise in the number of sectarian assassinations. This was an arrangement within the city, an attempt to provide a suitable population for what it had become. It required those who were alert to exclusion.

This was a good time for the Resurrection Men. They were seen as favoured and visionary. Defenders of the faith. Victor himself was rarely seen. Sometimes he would get Willie to drive him around. He talked about replacing the windows of the Capri with smoked glass. He was surrounded by rumour and speculation. It was said that he spent his days in a darkened room. It was said that he suffered under a meticulous foreknowledge of his own death.

In the end Coppinger compiled a list of their names with ease.

'It's amazing,' he told Ryan. 'You've just got to walk into a bar and people are pointing them out to you.'

He added that he had approached his editor with the names. Crommie, Barnes, Lambe, Kelly.

'I got all this trial by newspaper shit. The man says that if everybody's so sure it's them then why aren't they locked up. I got to remind myself that this editor started out reporting schoolboy hockey matches part time, for fuck's sake.'

To Ryan at that moment the reporting of local hockey matches played in a fading light seemed like a worthwhile and hardwon task with the virtues of endeavour, well-tended pitches, and the hallucinatory glimmer of white shorts against a darkening sky. But Coppinger went on to say that the identities of the men had been known to the police for a long time but that he had underestimated the degree of craft they brought to the killings. The carefully chosen routes, the stolen cars that were burned afterwards to destroy evidence, the removal of lead particles from clothing. He thought that the whole patient methodology was written down and stored in a locked filing cabinet. There would be pathology reports, photographs of victims, photographs of the Resurrection Men themselves; black and white shots, taken from a concealed camera, of men who could have been mafia or drug smugglers caught unaware in poses of artless evil. He said they operated across different police divisions in the knowledge that co-operation between divisions was minimal. Operations were hampered by distrust of the police. Detectives hinted at threads of sympathy for the killers in the lower ranks. There seemed to be a dark current of approval in the political sphere.

Coppinger seemed to be driven by this information. Ryan began to wonder what private purpose was served by this fascination. There was no doubt that it was a theme which rose above the ordinary violence of the city. One of the rare happenings which declared itself different, yielded to appraisal, demanded a new agenda. Still this did not account for Coppinger's obsession. Ryan had noticed that the other man had developed a bad smoker's cough. The fingers on both hands were yellowed and he was paying less attention than ever to his dress. His cough came in long cancerous bursts, instantly recognizable in a bar or at a crime scene. There seemed to be a formal structure to it. And the more he coughed the more he smoked. Untipped Gallagher's Greens. He seemed to cling to it, and Ryan could see its heroic qualities, the refusal to move warily in the presence of his own dying.

Coppinger wrote out the names for him and stuffed it into his breast pocket. He found himself taking it out frequently and surveying it. Ivan Crommie, Ian Barnes, William Lambe, Victor Kelly. He could not connect with them. They had the insubstantial feel of men listed missing in action.

That summer he thought that his marriage was still somewhere in the city, stored intact with its pleasures and accumulated loss. In the evening he would walk through the city centre to Charley Lavery's and sit at the bar drinking slowly, watching couples behind him in the bar mirror, their expressions like masks of recorded behaviour fitted to their faces. Studies of desire and anger. One night after he had left he saw a young couple who had been drinking there all evening. They were trying to cross Shaftsbury Square, the girl running ahead, grabbing things to stop herself falling. They were shouting at each other. Words of haunting blame and violence. The closing-time crowd watched them patiently. Two members of a police foot patrol looked on from a doorway. The boy fell over a car stopped at traffic lights. He turned and kicked the bumper and cursed at it. It was an intrusive presence in the mysteries of his anger. If he had been asked then why his marriage failed Ryan would have said incomprehension and the failure to grasp what was constant in his own heart. The boy and girl reached the other side of the square. Ryan listened to their voices trailing off into the distance, a note of surprise in their quarrelling, a sense of having discovered one of the many uses of love.

A week later he found himself in front of Heather's house. There was a crack in the front door glass patched with tape. The garden was unkempt. This was the way the house proclaimed its lifetime of many lettings, tenants changing two or three times a year. The house had accumulated their departures, their restless nights, their declining fortunes. The doorknocker hung from a bent nail.

He knocked on the door and waited, wondering what had brought him there. He did not expect Heather to open the door. She would have left and the new tenant would open the door, accustomed to these incursions. A girl with wet hair perhaps, hurried and resentful. A girl with fine bones framed by the hall-light, by the smell of cooking and the sound of a television. She would see him as a threat to her lightsome and temporary structure of home.

When Heather opened the door it was a moment before he recognized her. She was dressed in jeans and a sweatshirt and wore no make-up. He thought she looked like someone else's wife and suddenly saw another man coming to Margaret's door, drawn by something under the skin, a chastened beauty that was the sole and guarded preserve of the disappointed wife.

But this was not the reason he had difficulty in recognizing her. There had been some other change. Her body still possessed the same light bulk that suggested aerial properties but there was fatigue in her eyes as though she had spent hours in hopeless watching. She had the distant look of the fatally unnerved. She smiled vaguely at him then turned and walked down the corridor leaving him to follow.

When he reached the living room she was sitting on the

sofa beside another man. A television was on in the corner. The room contained the elements of a familiar domestic scene, the sum of achieved moments. Matching vases on the mantelpiece, a polished table, a gathering of possessions in a dim, familiar light. It was a small-town room, Ryan realized, taken aback by the richness of its own applied comforts. The souvenir ashtrays and Delft candlesticks had an air of having earned their sentiment and the right to sit apart, to be lifted daily and dusted, to be always in the margin of a woman's eye and beloved.

The man on the sofa seemed to be part of these arrangements. A man who worked with his hands perhaps. A panel beater, a fitter in a small engineering works. Ryan thought of him coming home in the evenings, washing his hands carefully with Swarfega, eating dinner and later in bed reaching for his wife carefully with those tended and fragrant fingers. He was smiling at Ryan. It seemed that he appreciated his surroundings and was happy to share the benefit of their stored, domestic virtue.

'You going to introduce me to your friend, Heather?' he said.

'This is Ryan,' she said, without taking her eyes from the television.

'And what does Mr Ryan do?'

'I'm a journalist.'

'Good, good.' Ryan felt that he was being reassured. That there was a procedure to be undergone in this room but that it would be simple and painless.

'My name's McClure,' the man said, reaching out his hand without getting up.

'Get us a drink there, Heather,' McClure said. Ryan sat down on an armchair as Heather went out. McClure didn't speak and Ryan felt that he was under intense scrutiny. He wondered if McClure knew about his encounter with Heather in the Harbour bar. He no longer thought that the man was boyfriend or husband. It was starting to feel like a pre-arranged meeting. There were unknown resonances. He felt that anything he said or did would be full of significance.

'She's a fine big woman,' McClure said softly, nodding towards the kitchen doorway. His tone implied that Heather was at a threshold, part of a species facing extinction, and that any reply would have to take the form of sorrowful agreement. Again Ryan could not find the words to answer, although McClure nodded as if he had, then looked at him as though to confirm that talk here would not be easy, that words would be cumbersome and fraught but must be exchanged none the less.

Heather returned with an unopened bottle of vodka and three glasses. She poured vodka into each glass, lifted one and sat down again facing the television. This made Ryan more uncomfortable. It seemed she intended to take no part of this, that she was estranged from what might follow.

'What do you work at yourself?' Ryan asked.

'Typical reporter,' McClure said, 'always on the job.'

'Just curious.'

'One thing and another. Communications you might say. A sort of a technician.'

'What, like television?'

'I fix things.'

McClure went to the television and switched over to the news. They watched in silence. This was an established ritual of the city. The news reports had acquired a new pattern. The newsreader's voice had a terse, censored quality, mixed with stern resolve. The emphasis had switched from coverage of riots and action shots of bombs exploding. The imagery was passive now. Blood-soaked pavements, booby-trapped cars covered with plastic sheeting. There were funerals, recurrent motifs of mourning.

When it was over McClure turned to Ryan.

'What do you think about these boys turning up with the throat cut?'

'Don't be starting that,' Heather said. 'Honest to God you'd think he could talk about nothing else.'

'Keep your beak shut, you. Is it somebody that's mad in the head doing it do you think?'

'I used to think that,' Ryan said.

'What do you think now?' McClure sat forward in his chair. Ryan felt that this was the reason he was here.

'Not mad exactly.'

'What are they then?'

'You get a feeling that it's done for a reason. They take pains over it. To frighten people. To show they can do it. To claim the town for themselves. Fuck knows.'

'It frightens you anyway,' McClure said softly, 'but the rest of you newspaper boys don't think a wild lot of it. Inside pages job so it is. Stick it in beside the small ads if they'd half a chance.'

Ryan shrugged.

'Let me tell you something,' McClure went on. 'We're all friends here, but the Protestant people have had enough so they have. Enough talk about rights and all. There's a question of a birthright being sold out here. Put that in your newspaper. We're the boys built the Empire and got a kick in the arse for it. Write about that. Ulster loyal and true. That's a thing to die for. We're all friends here, doesn't matter what foot you kick with in this house, but we'll not stand idly by for much longer.'

It was a speech Ryan had heard often. The same wintry tone. Words delivered to men in stiff suits under a doom-laden sky. It had the defiant note of a hymn sung in adversity. It conveyed the necessary spirit of a suffering people looking for succour, their voices grim and laden. But Ryan thought there was something fraudulent in McClure's delivery, a tone of mockery.

He noticed how submissive Heather was in McClure's presence. He was painfully deferred to. She was assiduous in her humility and McClure encouraged the impression that amends were being made for some old wrong.

When they had finished the bottle of vodka McClure suggested that they go out for a drink. Heather went out to change. When she came back into the room McClure looked her up and down, an attentive feminine glance attuned to mortal tirednesses.

'If a woman that size fell on you,' he said deliberately as she reached them, 'you'd be a long time getting up.'

Ryan remembered feeling good walking down the street towards the Supporters Club, Heather's arm linked through his, the world's rainy surfaces and reflections, passing lit shop windows offering the likelihood of life being there for the taking. It was moments like these that he worked towards in his drinking, when he could suppress the reflex to think badly of himself. In the bar McClure introduced him to other men from the Shankill and the Village, stocky men with tattoos showing on their forearms and some old darkness lingering in their brown, disinterested eyes. Ryan sat with Heather in a corner beside a poker machine while McClure stood at the bar talking. An hour passed. She asked him about his marriage, its singular labours and durable enmities. In small ways she let him know that the man that she had referred to was still around and that things were not going well. He felt that by talking to him she was equipping herself for hurt, that she did not intend to travel lightly in the proximity of disenchantment. He also began to sense that somehow knowledge of this man constituted dangerous information not to be entrusted to words. It had to be conveyed in cautious silences and significant looks. He knew that this silence was the great gift of the city, an enduring monument shaped in a mute effort of years.

McClure came back to the table.

'Babes in the wood,' he said, grinning at them. It was the way they must have looked from the bar. Huddled together, offering fairy-tale comforts to each other. Ryan straightened up, lurching slightly. He was aware of McClure's attention on him.

'That must be some feeling,' McClure said, making a motion of cutting his own throat. 'Cut clean to the bone. You'd wonder what class of a man would do that.'

His gaze was intent now, with a primal stillness. What was it that Ryan was being asked to share in? The victim's last moments, disbelief giving way, overwhelmed by a sudden terrible shyness? So much blood. Or the killer's feelings? The knife. The clarity. The silence of millennia.

When he looked again McClure had disappeared into the crowd and Heather was tugging at his arm.

'Come on, let's get the fuck out of here.'

He was vague about the rest of the evening. They went back to her house where she opened another bottle of vodka. She went to the window several times at the noise of a car outside. Soft, unhappy talk. Their loneliness seemed to fill the middle of the room, massive and sculptural, something you felt compelled to circle, examine, discuss its purposes in hushed tones. She avoided the subject of her lover, and when Ryan asked her about McClure she turned a face on him suggestive of lurid grief and he did not pursue it. She jumped at small noises and kept the lights turned low. As he got drunker Ryan found that he too began to experience moments of panic, a horror that felt artificial as if the night had been contrived towards this end. This type of fear, he realized, would be a speciality of a man like McClure. Gothic, manufactured. There was a cinema feel to it. Shadowy pursuing figures. The indistinct face pressed to the window. Heather clutching his arm nervously.

He woke at dawn. He was lying fully clothed on the sofa. He had the feeling that someone had just left the room. He walked into Heather's bedroom but she was asleep under the covers, her clothes on a chair in an unformed and intimate tangle he wanted to touch. He looked in the other rooms but there was no one there. The front door when he went to it was ajar. There was a grey mist and drizzle. He left closing the

door behind him. He had never liked dawn and its drama of
unpromising days.

By lunchtime he needed a drink. He found Coppinger at the
bar in Robinson's.

'You been keeping some strange company.'

'What does that mean?'

'I hear tell you were in the Supporters Club last night.'

'What about it?'

'With Billy McClure. You haven't a baldy have you?'

'What are you on about?'

'You look like shite. You look about ninety years old. Like
an old man with the shakes dribbling on to his shirt. Every time
you open your mouth, Ryan, I keep expecting disconnected
reminiscence, fucking senility, mistaking me for someone in
your childhood. You should never have left that wife of yours.'

'She threw me out. Who's this McClure anyhow?'

'Is your fucking arm broke or are you going to pay for that
drink? There was another knife killing while you were socializ-
ing last night. A barman on his way home from work. The throat
slit. Marks on the arms consistent with them being raised in
defence.'

'I thought McClure was strange. He kept watching me all
the time, mocking like.'

'When they found the poor fucker's body the arms were
folded across his chest the way you lay out a corpse.'

'McClure. I woke up on a sofa this morning with the feeling
that somebody had been watching me.'

'McClure is Mr Sinister. Connected to incidents involving
molestation of residents at several boys' homes. Links with
the British Intelligence establishment and several right-wing
head-case groups. Active in Protestant paramilitary circles but
not thought to be a member of any organization. Blackmail,
extortion. The name keeps coming up. Nobody says as much,
but there's hints that he's being protected in some way.

Witnesses retract statements. The word is that the peelers threw shapes at going after him a while ago but nothing happened. Not so much prevented from above but a certain disapproval was made known. So I'm just wondering here what the fuck you were doing having a quiet chat with him in the Supporters Club?'

'I wasn't doing anything with him. He was just in the company. This girl I met.'

'If he was drinking with a journalist it means he's got some use for you.'

'I'm telling you, the first time I ever saw the man.'

'What did you talk about?'

'Coppinger, I'm telling you I was clean drunk out of the mind. Could've been talking about anything. I remember he gave me this no surrender speech, Ulster loyal and true.'

'Who's the girl?'

'I met her at home. The da's funeral. I called over to her house last night.'

'This can't be coincidence.'

Ryan could see that Coppinger was impressed. He was looking on him with a new respect as if he had just been told of a dark event hidden in Ryan's past or found out that he had carried a secret burden through the years they had known each other.

'There's talk that McClure is connected in some way to the knife killings,' Coppinger said.

'He kept bringing it up last night. Asking what kind of a man would do something like that. It was like a challenge. Asking me was I that kind of man.'

'I'm worried the way he went to you.'

'There was this glint in his eye. You get the feeling that he knows more about you than he's letting on. But there's something fake in it too. He's acting a part. The sinister paramilitary. Letting things hang in the air. You start to feel unsure around him, out of your depth. He's letting you know you're part of things that you don't understand.'

'I'm beginning to think that the knife killings don't belong any more.'

'What do you mean?'

'The whole thing's changing. You see the way everything in this city is slipping down the news. Third item, fourth item. It's like there's a cultivated boredom out there. Another bomb, another dead UDR man. People's learning to switch channels when they hear it. I mean there's no good riot footage any more. The thrill you get when you see a petrol bomb hitting a Land-Rover. It gets harder and harder to make the headlines. The technology is changing too. Electronic surveillance, body-heat detectors, helicopters with nitesun searchlights. Nitesun. The confidential telephone, infra-red night 'scopes. There's a new vocabulary. Acceptable levels of violence, seven-day detention orders, the men of violence. It's like the whole thing's under control now. More than that, it's being ordered, contrived even. The Resurrection Men don't belong in it. Too unpredictable. There's a frontier air about them. Like a boom-town madness. Things that happen in lawless towns on the edge of the wilderness.'

'Saying you're right, where does me meeting McClure come into it?'

'Well, look at the way the thing's just starting to creep into the papers. It's a matter of time before there's an article every day with full-colour picture, English papers ringing up looking for long considered pieces, pile on the deprived background and all. You'll see the politicians going public on it. And that fucking name. The Resurrection Men. It's only a matter of weeks before you start to see the phrase "evil monsters", see it written in full tabloid headline. I think a decision's been took somewhere to get rid of them and I think that's what your man's at. He's making contact. He wants to lead you towards them, expose them.'

'If I get my throat cut you can have an exclusive.'

'I'm not on the story any more. It got took off me.'

'You're joking me. You've been on it for years.'

'They tell me I'm too involved. Can't be trusted to be impartial. I think it proves my theory.'

'Won't toe the line.'

'They're moving me to the sports desk. I know fuck-all about sports except for football. What does also-ran mean?'

'This is great. I've got this mad head McClure after me and you'll be doing the late results from Chepstow.'

'I'll nose around the place, find out what I can. I'll start with the woman. What's her name?'

'Heather Graham.'

'That's a good small-town Protestant name. Bet she's got the hair dyed blond, big headlights.'

'I was drunk. I just buried the da. I was feeling vulnerable.'

'You met her in this bar. She was drinking Pernod and blackcurrant. Or vodka and orange. Some sweet, sickly drink with plenty of alcohol.'

'It was Bacardi and coke.'

'You reminisced. The closed-down cinema. Taking girls up into the dunes. You said you were down for the funeral. You wanted her to feel sorry for you. You said your marriage was over.'

'This isn't funny.'

'A cheap appeal to the emotions. You groped her in the car park afterwards. She wasn't that keen but you made her feel she had led you on and she had to.'

'Listen, just cut out all that shite and find out something about her for me. I don't like this attention. They're probably cooking up a bomb for me under my car. Something with a mercury tilt switch.'

'Hurrying home through deserted streets. The smell of her perfume and that feeling of mystery you got when you were young.'

Back in the flat he thought about what Coppinger had said. That was what it came down to. A boy's sense of available mystery. A small town fixed in a lifetime of its own allurements. Arcade lights. Summer bandstands. It was what he looked for in women, disappointed when they proved themselves capable, accepted secondary satisfactions in the name of living, made the best of things, refused the offer of concealed positions within the heart.

His father loved the town. As he said this he would look sideways at his wife. It was an act of defiance. Proclaiming his life as a series of tawdry and irreversible journeys through its small streets. The town was enough for him, with its landmarks of decline, small incomes, infidelity. He remembered how his father's face had looked in death. The air of quiet satisfaction. Perhaps his mother had been correct in her attitude and his dying had been just one more small act of deceit and revenge. When Ryan thought of heaven as a child it was as a place where the dead stood in line for forgiveness.

He knew that his father had boasted in bars of his son the journalist, claiming an unearned credit for raising him. Or perhaps the man felt that he was providing a necessary sense of absence. What fathers are for. Their wandering. Their vivid lives.

Ryan was standing at the upstairs bedroom window with a glass of Bushmills in his hand. The city sloping down from the mountains to the lough. Divis, Tigers Bay, the Bone, the Short Strand, the Village, the Pound, Mackies, Shorts, Harland and Wolff. The city in all its history devised as a study in death. The shipyard that built Dreadnoughts. Engineering the means for people to face death. The ghettoes barely separated. The aspects of death common to any city. The lonely dying of pensioners. The monumental dying of public figures.

He expected McClure to contact him again. The man had a medieval air about him. The messenger whose coming presages famine and plague. It was an hour for uneasy imaginings, looking out over the ritual dark of the city. It felt as if there was something lying in wait for him out there, a prefigured end. The knife killers were taking shape and he was being drawn towards them. It seemed that the city itself had decided to devise personality for them, assign roles, a script to accompany a season of coming evil.

seventeen

Willie Lambe did not at first believe that he could carry out an operation on his own. It required a sense of timing and control which he did not believe he possessed. There were levels of fear to be maintained. When he did the first one it seemed ragged and barely in control and he found himself wishing that Victor was there. But even then Victor had started to take on the sleepless and haunted look of a man stumbling among the appalled belongings of his soul. The light in the back room of the Pot Luck sometimes burned all night which reminded Willie of ordeals endured on a sickbed by his father. Billy McClure described this to him as a pain of leadership. McClure was present when Victor asked Willie to carry out the next operation. Victor said it was necessary to continue to sow the seeds of blind panic among the Catholic population. McClure said that they were acting in defence of the Protestant population, its aims, ambitions and recognized virtues.

Willie was worried that Victor had an illness. His mother had told him that the city stood on a former marsh and that the ground you put your foot on was steeped in ailments of the chest. As a child he had nightmares of sickly vapours rising. When he was young his ambition was to be a doctor curing people with wisdom and touches of his admirable hands. He would tell the world how much he owed to a firm upbringing in the absence of a father. He would buy his mother a house on high ground away from the threat of eternal damp. When he told his mother this ambition she looked at him as if he had a defect.

When Big Ivan came down to the bar that day to say that Victor wanted to talk to him he admitted to a small feeling of dread. Victor had been uneven in his temper recently; however, Willie had great sympathy. He knew better than the others who were not overendowed in the understanding department. He saw the strain of command which left a man looking older than his years. He had been at Victor's right hand since the start and he knew that being given his own mission was a reward for loyalty. He could see the looks of respect on the faces of men in the bar. A person of standing which was what he always wished. Perhaps even his deeds seen in the light of history along with other defenders of the faith. A position involving your face on banners and songs about you in the clubs at night. In the end it did not come easy to him as he was by no means a person of natural cruelty. They lifted this Taig on the Newtonards Road who struggled against them which meant the use of blunt force. The fact was that this put his nerves on edge. There was the return of a twitch on the side of his face not seen since schooldays when it was an earner of nick-names. He made himself think about what the future held, perhaps driving along in an executive car as a trusted lieutenant, and this returned him to calm thoughts. Big Ivan confirmed Willie's impression of him that he had no wit by making jokes on the one hand and hitting your man at the same time. He found himself in sympathy with the man they had lifted, and it crossed his mind that afterwards they would go for a drink and share thoughts about the night, finding themselves in agreement about the behaviour of Big Ivan. He knew however that this was not to be and felt a kind of sorrow for those alone in the world.

The journey seemed to take a long time although it was only a few minutes. It often happens that a road you know well seems endless. It was a relief to his mind when it ended. He got out and went to the boot for the knives, leaving the others to move the man. It occurred to him standing at the back of the car that he was like someone on a mission of mercy in a location far from help. It was a place of broken street-lights and lonely rain. He walked back towards the man who was now on the ground. He felt himself overcome by reluctance at that point. He did not want to go through with it and later made statements to that effect, adding that in his opinion the finger of blame lay with Victor Kelly and no other. He thought of going back and reporting the mission accomplished but he knew that Victor would not be fooled and then he bent over and cut your man's throat on the ground.

It was after this incident that his mother began to look peculiar at him. A look like there was something in the distance that she couldn't make out. A look for things a long way off but coming your way.

In his opinion this and other actions were at all times under the directions and orders of Victor Kelly who must bear responsibility. He would say further that at that time everybody went in fear of Victor and there was no gain to be had in resisting his orders.

Victor had not driven his own car for months. Big Ivan or Willie Lambe took the wheel and he sat in the back. Often he would make them drive around the same streets for hours. He told them it was to do with the power he had acquired. It had to be displayed. He had decided that it answered a need in people, a craving for matters of opulence and dread. They always drove slowly with the engine idling in third gear. He wanted passers-by to think of curbed forces. Victor would stare straight ahead, his expression stern and commanding. He wanted to give the impression of someone contemplating harsh but necessary measures, a general with braid on his shoulders and dark glasses.

But sometimes on one of these runs he would say, where are we? He sounded surprised as if he had suddenly dis-covered that the streets were not the simple things he had taken them for, a network to be easily memorized and navi-gated. They had become untrustworthy, concerned with unfamiliar destinations, no longer adaptable to your own purposes. He read the street names from signs. India Street, Palestine Street. When he spoke them they felt weighty and ponderous on his tongue, impervious syllables that yielded neither direc-tion nor meaning. Sandy Row, Gresham Street.

When this happened they would return to the Pot Luck and Victor would go off to the back room with the razor-blade and mirror without a word, leaving orders not to be disturbed. After taking a line of speed he would attempt to sketch portions of the city, working fast and silent, streets discarded, corrected, gone over again and again until they yielded up names, faces. Each one seemed incomplete. More detail was required — people moved, discarded their occupations, emigrated, got lost. Whole streets were erased, expunged from records, fading into the curtailed memory of the elderly, a place subject to shortages and unexplained curfew where the recent dead seemed the least dependable of all.

It was during one of these periods that Victor killed Flaps McArthur. Flaps spent most of his days running errands for the Pot Luck unit. He had a low brow and undershot jaw and spoke with hesitation. Even a simple word was full of unexpected pitfalls as if his tongue and lips were an apparatus unsuited to the purpose of speech. His voice had a sinister, long-distance quality like a man speaking into a telephone receiver through a handkerchief. Everyday words acquired a muffled threatening sound. The nickname came from the way his ears stood out from the side of his head, huge and ornately whorled as if they belonged to a fabulous beast. Legendary feats of hearing had been ascribed to him. It was said that he had detected explosions on the border sixty miles away, conversations through locked doors. In the Pot Luck he occupied the role of a mascot. He was there from early in the morning until late at night, a mute and strange presence.

The suspicion had been growing in Victor's mind that information was escaping from the Pot Luck. Missions had been abandoned several times on coming across checkpoints. There were rumours that the police were planning raids in the area. One Tuesday evening he assembled the unit in the Pot Luck. When they arrived the stage at the back of the bar had been cleared and a chair was positioned in the centre with a single light shining on it. The men gathered at the bar. It was a plain wooden chair and during the course of the evening they began to look uneasily towards it, becoming aware of its chipped members and dull varnished surfaces. It was the kind of chair to be found in police stations, court buildings and other places designed to the specifics of public retribution. As the evening wore on and Victor still did not appear the significance of the chair grew on them. The spotlight illuminated an area of human absence and gave definition to it, boundaried in light with its dimensions revealed. At eleven o'clock Big Ivan came out of the back room and went behind the bar. He poured double vodkas for all of them, Victor's orders. They drank them quickly and ordered more. Biffo turned down the bar lights so their attention was focused on the cone of light in which the chair sat, contained and sufficient. Victor walked out of the back room carrying the Browning loosely in his right hand. By his face he was attempting to master a powerful emotion. He crossed the stage to the chair and stood behind it with both hands resting on its back. He paused, scanning the crowd to ensure that they had grasped the meaning of the chair. It was a place of last refuge. It was a place of utter solitude.

'We got a traitor,' he began quietly, 'an informer in our midst. A Judas. Our aim's been betrayed and our most inner thoughts made known.'

He spoke slowly and deliberately, allowing each word to stand revealed.

'There's an informer in this room,' he shouted suddenly. 'I hope the fucker's arms and legs wither. I hope he gets fucking cancer.'

He began to pace the stage, crossing and re-crossing the patch of light and gesturing with the pistol, head down, breathing hard. He was gathering their regard to him and giving shape to his fury.

'I been reluctant to admit that one among us has gone and sold his birthright.' His voice was soft again. He was talking in a style that his audience were accustomed to. The preacher's formal madness. The voice pitched and commanding. The vocabulary of flood and plague. The audience swayed now, attuned to themes of wrath and mercy. When Victor stopped talking there was absolute silence. Suddenly he raised the pistol and pointed into the front row.

'Come on up here, Flaps.'

Flaps looked at the men around him, blinking his eyes slowly and wetting his lips. He held his hands palm upwards in front of him, his uncomprehending stare fixed on Victor. He stood up slowly. The men behind him pushed him forward.

'Sit in the chair there, Flaps.'

'I never done nothing, Victor, swear to God.'

'Sit in the chair.'

He did as he was told. The audience looked on, convinced that this would be a spectacle of redemption and that Flaps would emerge from the ordeal, purged and godly. They would be stirred to pity by a stumbling confession and find themselves warmed in the end by the possibilities of redemption.

'Swear to God, Victor, I never, swear to God, Victor.'

Victor was walking round him now, studying him as if this were a matter of promising angles, and solvable by degrees.

'Swear to God, Victor,' Flaps said in a terrible, dry-mouthed whisper, his body trembling. His eyes were screwed shut but

Victor knew that he was capable of hearing a lethal approach. To McClure it seemed distant, a televised roadside execution coming intact from a far-off war. Victor placed the barrel of the Browning against the side of Flaps' head and fired a single shot, flat and undramatic, and Flaps fell sideways off the chair. No one moved. This must be a simulation of death, a poor rehearsal. Victor looked down at them. There were timely conclusions here for all of them, his face said, but they did not understand. He nudged Flaps with his foot.

'Get rid of this fucker,' he said, then walked off the stage towards the door of the back room. They exchanged puzzled glances then moved to do as he said, standing for a moment to gaze on Flaps' unconvincing corpse.

Several days later Victor had Willie Lambe drive him to his parents' house. Willie drove the car around the corner and watched the street after Victor went in. Victor was becoming increasingly aware of the possibility of assassination. He knew as soon as he opened the door that his mother was not at home. He walked down the hall to the kitchen, glancing at the pieces of furniture which had been carried from house to house until in the end they seemed to be imitations of furniture, unfixed and lacking in conviction. Victor went into the kitchen which was the only room that appeared unchanged no matter how many times they moved; not so much a room as the sum of what was well regarded by his mother. The tin of Vim under the big porcelain sink, the clothes line hanging on pulleys from the ceiling. A place of cooking and washing and watery legends prepared against the onset of sudden grief. His mother's shopping bag was missing from the hook behind the door. It was enough to bring a tear to his eye to think of her walking between the stalls at Smithfield market. A small figure in flat shoes and a tweed coat following a threadbare routine, weighing carrots with hands she thought of as blameless — thrifty and cautious in a way that was meant to show that she knew just how much can go amiss in a life.

He wished that she was here. He wanted to sit down at the kitchen table with her and talk about his life, reduce it to a series of wanly regarded incidents in the way that made her laugh until she would start to tell him things that he had done as a child, producing these memories shyly as proof that he held an honest place in a mother's beseeching heart.

When he was at school he used to hope that she would fall ill so that he could pay for an operation. He imagined selfless vigils by her bedside with nurses shaking their kindly, immaculate heads in admiration.

Sighing to himself he went to the back door and opened it. The pigeons in his father's loft were making their usual endless noise of intimate discovery. Victor lit a cigarette and looked up in time to see his father emerge from the doorway of the loft. They faced each other motionless across the yard as though a small pause was expected of them. For Victor, to study his father the way a child studies an adult with the frontal stare that is an entitlement of childhood. For the older man, to stare back, a father's guarded look aware that his role lies in the measured display of his shortcomings and in ascertaining which disappointments his child will find serviceable.

His father appeared to have grown smaller. There was grey stubble on his cheeks and he was wearing an old nylon shirt and blue overalls. It was a look he had deliberated over, a studied shabbiness which he had adopted. He had learned all there was to know about positioning himself against the unstable surfaces offered by the world in a way that made him invisible. He could avoid the sectarianism of the shipyard where he wished to be seen as inattentive to causes and to the kind of conscientious attention to suffering that had earlier that day led to workmates planting a bullet in a Catholic worker's lunch-box. He had seen the man lift the bullet out of the plastic lunch-box and adopt a studious expression as if he might extract some testimony regarding his eventual fate from its brassy and rigorous outlines.

'Your ma's not here.'

The sentence came out like a final repudiation of Victor who had remained in the kitchen doorway, red-eyed and haggard and tense as if he was about to mount a dark raid into the disputed territory between fathers and sons. James came across the yard and pushed past him into the doorway.

'You're too late. Your ma's not here,' he repeated as if this assertion was sufficient to fend off the terror and doubt that his adult child brought with him. Victor could sense this and was pleased by what he thought was a father's reluctance to hand over his place on the earth. But there was more to it than that. When his father had gone into the house Victor went across the yard and opened the shed door. The loft had been built on to the top of the shed with a trapdoor separating them. The shed hummed with a formed and various pigeon noise. Victor sat down on an old kitchen chair. Every house they had lived in had possessed a place like this, a lean-to with a dusty, eternal air, and Victor often sat in them when his father was at work. There were always the old electric fires, broken toasters, objects with a dull suggestive gleam. It seemed that disuse was a built-in part of their design.

At his feet there was an Outspan box full of newspaper cuttings. He lifted it on to his knee. He knew that his father would cut out anything to do with Linfield from the Newsletter. News of victory or defeat, manager profiles or transfer rumours. A detailed record from the humble origins of the club to its ascent through the league gathering lore to itself. A history you could use instead of a city or a family with its complex undocumented inheritance.

But these cuttings had nothing to do with Linfield. The top one had a photograph of Flaps with his name underneath. Robert Craig McArthur. There was an account of his body being found in a builder's skip with a single gunshot to the head.

Unnamed sources stated that he was involved with the group known as the Resurrection Men. Robert Craig McArthur. Victor had never known him as anything but Flaps and the full name gave his death an authority it hadn't possessed before. He emptied the box on to the floor. They were all there, named in full. McGinn, Curran, McGrath. Some underlined, others with a question mark beside them. Full names that spoke of an existence fully lived. He realized that a name was accomplished and haunting, and that having read them he could not divest himself of them but they would come to him again like an old pain coming intact through the innuendo of years.

eighteen

The parties in Heather's house had died out and she hadn't seen McClure since the night of Ryan's visit two months before. She spent most of the day in front of the television with the curtains drawn. She watched repeat serials, fixed on their moody and elegaic characterization. At night she examined her face in the bathroom mirror for signs of adequacy. She thought about herself at forty. Like one of those women you saw on Royal Avenue with big houses on the Malone Road. A wife well dressed and smelling faintly of alcohol. A wife who was crafted and apprehensive. Rich women comfortless in the knowledge of their marred, once-beautiful husbands. Before she had come to the city she had wanted it for herself. A thin voracious mouth and an aura of expensive suffering.

At night she had the feeling that she was living in a house belonging to someone else. She felt surrounded by a missing person's possessions. The cosmetics on the dressing table were unfamiliar. The clothes in the bedroom wardrobe seemed to belong to another woman. She found herself looking through the bottoms of drawers and behind wardrobes for evidence of the secret life that is craved in others. The yellowed letters, old banknotes, the dated pornographic magazine which catered for some longfelt pain. When she tried on clothes they seemed to have been bought for someone else. She imagined a plain sufficient body unlike her own with its tolerant poise, its air of having struck its bargains.

She missed Darkie. He hadn't been to the house for

months and McClure told her that he had disappeared. He's cracked up, McClure said, the head's gone entirely. He said he had seen Darkie with the winos at the bottom of the Lisburn road. He was wearing plastic bags on his feet, he said. Darkie had contacted her once but she hadn't mentioned it to McClure. The phone had rung in the middle of the night with a tone of imminent loss, of worst fears confirmed. When she answered it a voice she did not recognize whispered, 'Is he there?'

'Is who there? Who is this?'

'Victor, is he there?'

'He's not here, who is this?'

'Darkie, Darkie Larche.'

'Darkie, where the hell are you? I thought you were dead.'

'He's going to kill me.'

'Who's going to kill you?'

'Victor.'

'Victor's not going to kill you, Darkie. He knows you're my mate.'

'He said he would kill me.'

'Where are you?'

'I'm in a wet place. Heather, I went and drunk meths the other night. It tasted nice but I'm in a damp and drippy place. I'll catch my death.' He giggled.

'You're fucking drunk now.' But Heather realized there was more to it than that. She recognized it in his voice. The knowledge that there was something sinister abroad in the city. A surefooted presence in the shadows.

'You never come to see me no more, Darkie.'

'I can't. You don't mind the row we had in the bar, I told him he was a Catholic and all. Victor never forgets that. I'm a dead man. You wouldn't want a dead man to come calling,' he said sadly.

'Remember all the times we had together Darkie?'

'I don't remember nothing. There isn't nothing to remember.'

'I'll come and get you.'

'I'm away now, Heather.'

'Don't.'

Darkie was gone. She replaced the receiver with the feeling that she had failed him.

One morning she pulled back the head of her bed to find a microphone taped to the wood. Its head was greasy and disused and the wire leading from it had been severed.

Victor came round once or twice a week. He was morose and subject to sudden outbursts. He would check all the rooms when he came in and repeat this procedure during the evening. He complained of being spied on and peered through the curtains if he heard a noise outside. He told her that he had authentic fears for his safety. He said it was a case of trust nobody, although he mentally put Dorcas aside. McClure had told him about Ryan. Come sniffing round Heather, McClure said, looking for his hole. Victor said he wasn't worried. That he was still number one with policemen nodding to him at checkpoints. About you, Victor son. But he thought about it when he was in bed with her as she worked him towards the lasting amphetamine erection. When she did not succeed he distrusted her. The expression on her face said that she had returned to a long-held prerogative to be hapless in love but to count in her own heart when she was alone.

'You ever fucked a Taig?' he demanded one night. He didn't look at her when he said it but she felt herself being manoeuvred towards the edge of a dangerous solitude.

'I asked you a question.' He raised himself on one elbow above her and she remembered their first meeting when he had seemed like a foreigner, practised in lost crafts of menace, his thin lips opening to utter artful words of cruelty. He took her arms in a painful grip and looked at her thoughtfully and she realized that he could kill her. She imagined her naked body being found like a cover from *True Detective*. The abandoned limbs and parted lips, the pose arranged and lingered over.

'I wouldn't go near one in a fit, Victor,' she whispered. She thought calmly of the newspaper headlines following her death. Strangled with own stocking. Clothing in disarray. The wistful erotic overtones.

'What about thon fucking reporter? Did he dip the wick?'

'Somebody I knew from home. He just come up here, Victor. I never asked him or nothing.'

He stared at her for a minute then released her arms and lay down beside her again.

'No one you can trust. Even Willie and them boys, let you down a bagful. Act the big lad but they'd be fuck-all without Victor. Government knows about Victor, after him all the time and think he doesn't see them, plainclothes men. Give them the slip. Contacts in the law keep Victor informed. Victor's no dozer. Biding their time then shoot him down like a dog in the street. Lure you with women, drink, money. Bait the trap. They think Victor doesn't know their wee game. They think he doesn't laugh in their face.

'The Resurrection Men. They think they know what it means but they haven't a notion. They've got the head up their holes they don't know nothing.'

'What do you mean Victor?' Her throat was dry so that she could barely speak. Outside she could hear traffic, the sound of voices. Light fell across his face through a gap in the curtains. She felt that their three years together had evolved towards this lull, the feeling you got walking on your own down an empty street at night — a feeling of grey pavements and unlit pavements, a suspenseful and achromatic terrain where you strained to hear the cold sound of a pursuing footfall.

'Youse is the Resurrection Men,' she said finally. 'You and Big Ivan and Willie and Biffo. You done all them killings.'

He told her about it, laying stress on operational details and individual acts of bravery. He tried to describe what it was like leading men on a mission, a handpicked team working under the noses of the law. The feelings of comradeship. The way they all knew a target when they saw one, recognizing the victim's lonely charisma.

He said little about the killings themselves but he managed to convey the impression of something deft and surgical achieved at the outer limits of necessity, cast beyond the range of the spoken word where the victim was cherished and his killers were faultlessly attentive to some terrible inner need that he carried with him. Victor used the victims' full names. He told her how he found himself in sympathy with their faults and hinted that during their last journey he nursed them towards a growing awareness of their wasted years and arranged their bodies finally with an eye to the decorous and eternal.

Kill me.

Later when he was asleep Heather got up and went to the kitchen where she made tea and sat at the table in her nightdress. She had heard hundreds of stories about the knife murders. After each one there had been rumours about what they did to their victims. It reminded her of the periodic rumours about satanic rites in the old graveyard at home. Tombstones defaced, cats disembowelled, the presence of virgins. Lurid and necessary small-town fictions. It was said that the Resurrection Men wore pointed hoods and that they drained their victims' blood and drank it. She had been in the Eglantine Inn one night when a man who worked as a porter in the morgue at the Royal Victoria had described the limp, bloodless cadavers. People had crowded around him in silence. He spoke with a strong, gravelled voice full of authority and the crowd had approved of this. It was what they expected from someone who tended the dead.

She had always liked this time of night before. If she was with a lover it was a time for a factual domestic seriousness with long considered silences. If she was on her own she could sit and think, be wily with herself, and develop a sense of getting to the bottom of things. The house at night lent itself to that. Full of ticking silences with everything in its place and stilled so that you had room to be particular about yourself and your life.

But it wasn't working for her tonight. There was the distorted, uneasy silence of a horror film. Something was abroad that she didn't like. There was a scant rattling in the dry shrubs at the front door, a prowled quiet around the house.

She had always liked Victor's hands. To lie back and allow them to go where they wanted. They had a brevity of touch, skilled in nuances, that made you feel as if he was executing a flawless sexual design. Suddenly she pictured him crouched over a corpse holding a knife. The same intentness on his face that she saw in bed, seeking the pattern, the deep-set grain, with dreamy inventive movements. She got up from the table and walked to the sink where she was sick in a matter of fact way, abandoning herself to the rhythm of it.

She lay in bed beside him. She thought that if there was someone else in the room they could see the whites of her eyes like a picture of fear showing how she had made herself come back into the bedroom, take off her dressing gown, lie down. She was facing away from him, hoping that he wouldn't turn into her in his sleep, put his arm around her to hold her breast. A feeling she usually loved, replete and dozing. But not tonight. Not this night with the shadows gathering, darkness manifest.

nineteen

Coppinger had obtained the autopsy reports from the last two killings and agreed with Ryan that they had been carried out by a different person. The wounds were repetitive, unlike the earlier attacks where the injuries seemed somehow tailored to the age and status of the victim. There was evidence of carelessness, panic, reluctance.

The media coverage of the killings increased. The victims were profiled, their last movements traced. The minor details of their final hours were examined for signs of mishap or an unexpected involvement with fate. Neighbours spoke on television. Careworn women who managed the sentences of condemnation with care, exercising a vocal thrift. But the victims continued to emerge as being nothing out of the ordinary. It seemed that they insisted on it. The usual Friday night drink, small gains at the betting shop, routine ailments. This seemed to fuel public fear. No one wanted to be blamed for having lives of their own choosing and doing things that seemed marginal and slightly forlorn when those lives came under scrutiny.

Ryan wasn't asked to write on the subject. The task was assigned to senior staff reporters, men who wrote noncommittal reports which managed to sound burly and authoritative. He rarely saw Coppinger at the office. His sports reports were left in the postbox at night. Reading them Ryan found himself thinking about the disciplined solitude of a prison diary.

He was at home when Margaret rang. He had stopped going out to bars, preferring to bring home a bottle of whiskey. When he was drinking alone in the house he could work up to an impressive sense of ruined dignity. He had yet to take his first drink when the phone rang and he picked it up expecting to hear his mother's voice. No one else called him at home now.

'I thought I'd ring you,' she said. 'This friend of yours was round here earlier tonight.'

'What friend?'

'He sat for about an hour even after I told him you weren't living here any more.'

'Who was it?'

'I gave him a cup of tea.' Ryan realized that she would say who it was when she was ready, but that she wanted to determine the extent of his complicity first.

'He said he knew you well. I said how well and he started to imitate you. The way you hold your nose when you're thinking. He did that. It's not that I mind. He was funny.'

'Margaret.'

'What?'

'Did he have a name?'

'It was a Protestant-sounding name. Some wild Belfast name. You know like one of those names, when you say it, you have to screw up your face and squint like you'd a fag in your mouth. McClure, it was. Billy McClure. Called me missus all the time. Hi, missus, pass us a drop of thon milk there.'

'Listen, Margaret, can I come over?'

'I suppose so. When?'

'Now.'

'Right now? I don't see why not. Come on over, like.' She spoke the last sentence in an imitation of McClure's accent. East Belfast chant. Rising to a falsetto on the last word of the sentence with an intimation of fear.

*

Margaret opened the door wordlessly and walked behind him down the corridor humming. He felt that she should be nervous, bestow a long searching look. He expected her to acknowledge the estrangement they had worked at and maintained. To be equal to its nervous arts. He glanced into rooms as he passed but he no longer felt that any part of the house belonged to him, the furniture picked out between them in the early years of their marriage.

When they got to the living room she sat on the sofa with her legs curled under her. She didn't look at him, reminding him that all permissions had been revoked.

He sat in an armchair opposite her and told her about McClure. His undercover associations. The murders and his proximity to the Resurrection Men. His impression was that McClure was seeking him out. The quietness that descended whenever McClure's name was mentioned. The fatal hush.

He was leaning forward with his elbows on his knees. He felt that he had struck the correct pose, holding her eyes with his, using a measured tone. She was watching him as if he was performing a high-wire act with a tension in her eyes that was almost devotional, willing him across the great empty spaces between words. He watched her face. He realized that he had not considered how she would react to all this. He waited for her to curse him, reach for his face with her nails, throw him out along with the danger he had brought with him, along with the shirt he had worn for six days, the livid disarray of his life, the rank, outdoors scent of a former husband.

'Has he threatened you, this McClure?' Her voice showed an old concern left over from the years before they were married. He remembered late-night talks and his faltering confidences describing the miseries handed down by his father. Heirlooms of his house. He recalled the settings for these talks. The living room after her family had gone to bed, the huts on the beach, the back seat of a borrowed car. Places of luminous shelter where she tended his minor tragedies with thoughtful, unhurried sex. At eighteen the same serious attention to detail, the same determination to grasp what was worthwhile and proved in love.

'I was worried about you,' he said, 'when I heard that your man was over here.'

'No,' she said slowly. He could see her reviewing McClure's visit in her mind. 'No, I don't think it's got anything to do with me. When I think about it he seemed excited, but I don't think it's got anything to do with me.'

'He's killed people, mutilated them. He came up with the Romper rooms. He invented a form of communal assassination and called it after a children's programme.'

'He sat where you're sitting and admired the house. Where I got the wallpaper, how hard it is to keep a light-coloured carpet. He asked how long we'd been separated. It was, like, a kindly question, how hard the world can be and it's not anybody's fault. But most of all he talked about you. How he liked your journalism even though you're a Catholic. "From the other side of the house" was the way he put it. He said that he was worried about how much you were drinking. The point is that it was all to do with you.'

'He knew that you'd ring me. It's a way of telling me how much he knows about me.'

'Did you have anything to eat this evening?' she asked suddenly.

'The problem is I haven't a baldy what he wants with me. Why all this attention.'

'Did you eat anything today? This week maybe?'

'Half the time I think he's leading me towards something serious and half the time I think he's just playing with me.'

'If you told me you were coming I could have got food in.'

Like his mother she had insisted on food and mealtimes. It had added to the murderous churlishness he had felt like muscles balled under the skin. But once they had separated he began to see sense in the way the two women thought about meals. Skills of the kitchen, the handing-down of recipes, the use of linen. He saw that they were right in their attention to foodstuffs; he saw them moving gravely in the kitchen, involved in the ornamented passage of food to the table. Drawing out the theme of order, the theme of necessity.

She laid the table in the living room and ate with him. They spoke little. Remarks about their jobs, repairs needed to the house. When the meal was over they talked about friends and acquaintances — each name produced and news of each added carefully, their lives inspected for damage or unrest.

'I never got talking to you properly at the funeral,' she said finally. Her tone was careful. He realized that she was watching him closely, fearful of one of the silences he had worked into the fabric of the marriage until they had only wan common-places with which to gauge the extent of their failure.

'I mean you never really talked about what you felt, your da and all.'

He thought back to the day before the funeral when they had stood outside the house. Strangers, seen at a distance. Their mute, pained faces barely discerned. Their movements weighed down by an inaccessible personal history.

'All I felt was that I should have felt more.'

'You must have felt something. You were away with it. There was no talking to you. All you could feel was strain coming off you.'

'It wasn't really like he died. It was like he just ran off. Sneaked off. It wasn't like death, like gone for ever. It was as if he was in some other place, walking around pleased with himself.'

Across the table Margaret was supporting her head with her hands under her chin, her eyes full of the urge to revelation. He could see the small hairs on her arms, the delicate vein structure, the slightly moist creases in the crook of her elbow. It seemed a prayerful pose. He imagined dipping his face in the angle of her elbow, smelling a scrubbed, celibate fragrance. Here was a woman who did not wear perfume, who bathed after sex, who was scrupulous with regard to the world and its details. He remembered that when she was young she would always write her name in full. Margaret Elizabeth Clarke. It was a full account of herself. He wondered was this what lay at the bottom of her questioning about his father's death. A desire that she or anyone belonging to her should not leave unfinished business behind them.

'You can't tidy it up,' he said, 'you can't make it neat or just end it. I can't tell what I feel, I don't know.'

'OK, OK.' She covered his hand with hers. He sat with his head bowed. Fathers go on, he thought. They endure and accept blame in their memory. They refuse forgiveness to their own fathers. They invent their lives full of incident and hand them on for the instruction and punishment of sons.

The telephone rang at 3 a.m. News of the sleepless. He crossed the living room from the sofa and went into the hallway. Margaret's bedroom door was open. He could see the edge of the bed and a hand flung out. She always slept easily and deeply with an air of just reward. These hours of rest vouchsafed to herself. He walked slowly. He knew that the phone would not stop ringing before he reached it. It rang with a tone of imminent loss. As soon as he picked up the receiver he knew that it was McClure. There was a pause before he spoke in which Ryan could hear traffic noise in the background.

'Staying over at the wife's?' McClure said. His tone suggested that this was predictable, that he had long ago fathomed Ryan's motives and found them mean and everyday.

'What's it to you?'

'Couldn't blame you. Nice tits on her.'

'Leave her out of it, McClure. She's got nothing to do with it.'

'Everybody's got something to do with it.'

'What do you want?'

'I got a bit of information for you.'

'What is it?'

'There's going to be arrests.'

'Who's going to be arrested?'

'The Resurrection Men. Some of them anyhow. They're going to be lifted some time this next week.'

'How come you know?'

'People tell me things. I got a sympathetic ear.'

'What do you want me to do about it?'

'Anything you want, Mr Journalist. Point is they're not lifting the big man.'

'Who's the big man?'

'Fuck me, you really don't know, do you?'

'How should I know?'

'You've got a lot in common. Two of you like meat on your woman.'

'Fuck does that mean?'

'I'll be in touch. I'll tell Heather you were asking for her.'

McClure hung up. Ryan sat down on the floor, still holding the receiver. The night suddenly seemed full with as much cold promise as it could possibly hold. The telephone emitted a low note. He felt drawn into a dextrous conspiracy but felt the certainty that he would be there to witness what happened and nothing more. A minor figure not admitted to the benefits of tragedy. He felt manipulated; McClure had recognized the part of his life given over to the smallest kind of anticipation and meanness in the face of others' pain. A man who came to his former wife's house to trouble her with the residuals of love. There was something he had missed in the reference to Heather. He saw himself drawn to a type of woman who would recognize that her time with a man was limited and be dignified about it so that whatever end it came to would be fitting and sufficient.

After a few minutes he walked back down the corridor and stood at the doorway to her bedroom looking in. Light fell across the bed. At first he thought she was asleep, her body gathered under the bedclothes. A thoughtful arrangement of her limbs contrived for serenity. But as he began to move away she sat up quickly, pushing her hair out of her eyes.

'Who was it on the phone, your man McClure?' He nodded. She drew her knees up to her chin and studied him.

'What did he want?'

'He was giving me some information is all.'

'What are you supposed to do with it?'

'I don't know. I feel like I'm being asked to take part in something. All of a sudden I'm part of a conspiracy. I feel like I could be arrested.'

'That's a bit dramatic.'

'Maybe. Coppinger was saying about the courts here, the way they are. No juries, evidence being given behind screens by unidentified witnesses – soldier A, soldier B, that kind of thing. The strange charges they come up with. Conspiracy with persons unknown to murder persons unknown. I was arguing it was a denial of justice. Coppinger says it's all just a mechanism for dealing with different forms of complicity. He says this town has invented new ways of getting involved, like it's all just one big experiment in human guilt.'

'He called round the other night.'

'What sort of form was he in?'

'Acting all jovial. He looked tired, worn out. He kept falling asleep, just dozing off in the middle of a sentence. We'd both pretend he wasn't doing it. He's got cancer.'

Ryan felt himself adjusting his face towards disbelief, picking out the elements, a passage of emotion recollected with difficulty.

'He's got it in the throat. Couple of months they told him. He didn't want me to tell you. Says you'd only call it a cheap metaphor. He thinks you'll laugh at him.'

'How long has he known about it?'

'He says only a few weeks. I think he's known for longer. I keep going back over time. He's been beating Rennies into him for months, and heartburn's a symptom.'

It fitted with Coppinger's demeanour over the previous year. The air of slow draining, of withdrawal. It was not like death in the city. That was wilful, to be opposed. It seemed that Coppinger was facing a death without dimension, a thing without qualities. Ryan thought about the coughing. He thought about Coppinger embarked into the noisome precincts of the dead.

'I feel like I only got to know him,' Margaret said quietly, 'and now he's different.'

'I wish he'd told me. I reckon he thinks I can't take it.'

'Maybe he just didn't want to hear you doing what you're doing now.'

'What's that?'

'Thinking about yourself.'

Margaret and Coppinger would have sat late into the night talking about him. Margaret bringing an industriousness to bear on the failure of their marriage. Coppinger accepting her confidences as dues owed to the dying.

'He says he's more scared of pain than he is of death. He wants to know, if he was really suffering at the end would somebody pull the plug, put a pillow over his face. I think he was just saying it. I got mad and said he'd no right and he just laughed at me.'

Coppinger attempting to change the nature of his dying by ringing it with deceptions, ironies, difficult questions. Already there were demands on their loyalties; elements of mystery and suspense.

'Please kill me.'

'What was that?'

'Nothing. It's near six. I think I'll go back to the flat.' Margaret nodded agreement. They both felt a growing sense of lingering in the ruins. The familiar outlines of blame were becoming visible. He could tell she was enervated, ready to howl for the state of love.

twenty

Dorcas felt her life disarrayed by the sorrows of Victor. There would be a burden of his unlived years through all her own days. She knew that the lies of government are a dagger but that there is no worse torment than the love of children. She was as a woman ruined and all goodwill had deserted her mind.

Of the events leading to the shooting of Victor she could recall only a little, owing it seemed to an obstruction in the memory. When she cast her mind back the sole things that came to her were heavy like a weight of sorrow. Such as the appearance of Victor in those days. Though she had seen him seldom she observed how the flesh had fallen from him and her heart misgave her. There seemed to be a knowledge of death untimely in his eye. In later years she persisted in the view that he gave himself for others and that at least was a gift of condolence.

There was one memory she would have liked to expel from her head. She awoke in the night with palpitations in the chest and a feeling that something was amiss. She came down the stairs beset by the same breathlessness to come across a strange scene in the living room. She was not the type of woman inclined to ghastly thought, but icy fingers was not the phrase for what she felt that night when she had seen her husband and her son at the kitchen table. It was like a sinful past come back to haunt you. She was in mortal fear to put one foot in front of another or open her mouth. Victor was sat at one end of the table and James at the other. Her tongue felt glued to the roof of her mouth like a useless tool. There never was an expression the equal of the one on Victor's face as he looked at his father. It was a stare of exact hatred for the wrongs that man done his family. She could see her son's torment with deep lines on the forehead and darkness under the eyes. James faced him with a like expression. It felt to her like being in a room where there has lately been a great tragedy which is now over but there are parts left to overwhelm the mind. They sat still, like statues or graven images, and did not look next or near her so that it was as if she had never been a party to either of their lives. If she had to put a word to what was in front of her eyes then that word was sundered and she felt like a witness summoned to watch.

The last of it was that Victor stood up from the table like a creature lifted against its will and turned towards the door without a word being spoken. He carried his body stiffly as though it was an injury to him and the tears were in her eyes ready to trip her as he closed the door behind him. She looked around the room to seek the usual comfort she had in the minor possessions that she had maintained through so many moves so that each place would bear the stamp of a respectable house. Nothing much more than souvenir delft and a few sticks of furniture polished daily and a few other items of sentiment. Often she felt that these ornaments alone stood between her and the road. She said often that they might as well live in a caravan as lift all up and flee every time they got settled. She said often to Victor that she never knew why she did not get a job as a packer of valuables for transport to distant lands.

It was while she was lost in this thought that James took to his feet and delivered himself of such a cry as froze her to the spot. It shamed her afterwards that a man could give voice to such a wilderness of noise that not even a woman would make in her belief. From a man who hardly strung two words together in all his born days. He turned to her with a desperate look and says he what did I do wrong but she did not move a mortal bone in her body towards comfort for him. She knew that if Victor had met her first that night he would have met solace and not a harsh stare that would tear the living flesh. She could have brought understanding and perhaps salvation from an eventual fate. She decided that from that day on he would not get daylight from her except food and clean clothing as it was not in her nature or upbringing to begrudge him that. She turned on her heel to him and went upstairs for a night of tossing and turning. When she came down in the morning he was gone to work with the dishes washed and a light put to the fire but if he thought he could win back what he lost with such things he had a mistake coming to him.

That night left her with a feeling of dread which left her listening to the wireless at all hours in case there was some word of Victor. When she heard the news of his friends Big Ivan and Willie and that man Barnes she knew that the finger of wrongful accusation would not stop there. There was no word from Victor then for many weeks and her heart bade her believe he had left the country. The advice she had ready for him was exactly that and it is hard circumstances that put the words leave the country for your own sake into a mother's mouth. She knew though that Victor would not leave. He was not the type to leave a friend in trouble or abandon the purpose of a lifetime.

Willie Lambe would confess that he had always had a fascination with knives, remembering his first one as a scout knife with a veneered wooden handle. He liked the weight of a knife in the palm, solid and assured. It gave you a sense of a task to hand. Here was a tool designed for basic materials. Wood, rope, cloth. Sometimes he would sit in his room for hours with the set of filleting knives and think about the story they could tell, the dark considered history retained in their shape. Often he carried them in the boot of his car and it gave him a secret pleasure to drive along with someone who did not know of their presence. He felt that they were all there was of mystery in his life.

He liked to take them along when he was driving one of the Pot Luck crowd about the city at night, driving fast along empty streets, or waiting outside some desolate house with only the glow of the interior light to assert that there was still some comfort a man could take from the night. Having the knives with him gave Willie a calm strength that made him seem open and unburdened to these men with the result that they talked to him, confessed ordinary sins, and asked him for advice. He thought about them the whole time, resting in slots in their wooden box. They were proof of his part in the events of the city and their bright, singular virtue enabled him to think of himself as equal to the world.

During this period he tried to spend as little time as possible at home. His mother rarely spoke to him but looked at him often in a narrow-eyed calculating manner as if he was being measured for some fitted garment of disapproval that she was preparing in another room. It scared him. He knew that she was capable of a vindictiveness which was expansive enough to take in all levels of your life and thought, all the more dangerous as age weakened her, so that retribution was the only scope for triumph she had left. He found that he even missed her denunciations of his father. She seemed to have lost the urge to lecture him about men and their shabby, impermament loves.

Willie did not know how she had discovered what he had been doing with Victor and the others, but he accepted that she knew. It seemed to him that the voices of the dead were accessible to her, one of the ghostly talents inherited by the aged. She spent most of the day alone in the sitting room now surrounded by her photographs, mementoes, letters, boxes he carried from the attic. She brought her prayer book, inscribed with the birth-dates of her parents, everywhere and carried out daily inspections of her mother's lace tablecloths and fine bone china. He shivered when he opened the door to find her sitting among these things with her eyes closed as if she had assembled a device with which to assess the cluttered thoughts of the dead, their portioned loneliness. He imagined his own name repeated in their whispered tales of consequence. Their arrival among matters of lamentation. The knives. The shadow that now occupied the places lost to them.

Big Ivan had only ever had his picture in the paper once. It was when he was eight years old and played in goal for the school team. He had kept the photograph which showed him standing in the back row with his arms folded. The team wore jerseys and shorts intended for older boys. Their heroic stance seemed equally ill-fitting. The back row standing on boxes, the captain with his foot on the ball. The whole composition had a strangeness to it – the smudged, awkward faces, the white fold-marks running through the paper, the sense that they are committed to a much grimmer task than football. He longed to have his picture in the paper again. He thought that it would reveal hidden public qualities. In prison he imagined the paper being passed around the bar in the Pot Luck, his enigmatic expression pondered, men trying to recall words that he had spoken, sorrow mixed with pride that he had gone from among them. People would look at his face on their way home from work or over an evening meal, feeling strangely stirred, saying here is a leader for society, a man confident with women. These were things he had seen in many photographs. Faces in the paper were different from faces you saw in the street. They had a look which said they were appointed by destiny to be there. He nearly cried of pride the time that Victor did Flaps and there was Flaps in all the papers the next day looking like someone approved by angels so that you would never think that the lift did not go all the way to the top floor. Big Ivan stared at Flaps and found it hard to credit the fact that he had never paid much mind to him. Flaps' gift of hearing seemed somehow visible. He went to several different bars that night and left the paper face-up on the bar so that he could say here is my friend Flaps in the paper, would you believe? Then he would watch as the person beside him examined the photograph. He believed that in this way people would be dead impressed, women and suchlike. He was therefore surprised when they all walked away as he began to talk so that he wondered if there was any respect left. By ten o'clock he felt locked with all the vodka he had drunk and fell into sad thought about the days he would drive about with Victor looking for Taigs to give a digging to.

Every day Biffo Barnes sat silent and unapproached at the table under the window in the Pot Luck drinking bottles of Smirnoff Blue which were placed without question in front of him. Those who watched him saw that his eyes were fixed on the door and that his lips sometimes moved strangely as though he were counting, as though his was a grim clerkship tasked with taking measure of the dead.

twenty-one

Even at dusk when the streets have emptied of traffic there is a sense of unendurable delay in the city, a faltering of purpose with solitude prevalent. Especially at dusk when the city admits an airy and marginal light from the sea. There are the tones of wet slate, rainy and measured textures sustained in car windscreens and office windows and it seems that nightfall is the least likely of all possible outcomes. The few people that are abroad walk uncertainly or linger until it appears that they have lost their memory of the city, or that the memory of the streets themselves has been damaged.

'They lifted Barnes out of the Pot Luck,' Coppinger said. 'Herbie, the CID man, walks in and Barnes stands up on the two hind legs and says, "You're fucking dead Herbie." Herbie says, "Is that right, Biffo?" and Barnes just laughs dead quiet and says, "That's right, Herbie, you're fucking dead, you just don't have the wit to stiffen."'

'That's just a story.'

He had been in bars and clubs all day, Coppinger told Ryan. The Gibraltar, Maxies, even the Pot Luck. He had heard dozens of stories about the arrested men. These were as yet unrefined, betraying their origins in older stories or in the adaptable myths of television. People coming to grips with the raw, untransformed facts of the Resurrection Men.

'All the talk is that Big Ivan Crommie is spilling the guts on the other two. Course he done nothing.'

When Ryan had arranged to meet Coppinger in Robinson's bar, Margaret had warned him about the physical change. He's getting transparent, she had said. But it was his face that disturbed Ryan. He no longer looked withdrawn. He had the look of an animal lured from cover by some terrible need.

'Big Ivan cries like a ba when the peelers get him into Castlereagh. Says he was just acting the big man. Wants to know if he'll be on television. Your man Willie Lambe's saying the same thing. Biffo Barnes, he never opens the mouth.'

'What gets me', Coppinger said, 'is Lambe having the knives right there in the back of the motor in this big case lined with velvet. Red fucking velvet. They're all refusing to name the man behind the whole thing. They say he'll kill them. See the paper today? They've took to calling him Captain X. It's like a comic. Mystery man Mr X. Evil monster. Next thing he'll be stalking the streets. That's what evil monsters are supposed to do. Stalk the streets hunting for victims. Is it cold in here or is it just me?'

'It's cold all right.'

'Don't fucking lie to me. I knew you'd come out with some corny lie. I was waiting for you to tell me I was looking well. You were always a corny bastard. I hear you went to see Margaret the other night.'

'That's right.'

'I hope she showed you the red card, she's away too good for the likes of you. Wasted my time trying to teach you anything. Put a fucking beggar on horseback. I can see you loving all that Captain X shit. I suppose you're waiting for the usual line about you getting back with Margaret. A dying man's last wish for you to agonize over. It'd appeal to your half-arsed sense of tragedy.'

'I saw Captain X written up on a wall already. There's the beginnings of a myth in there.'

'Paint's cheap.'

'Maybe so,' Ryan said, thinking however that the name Captain X supplied all that the city required in the way of fearful names. It was lurid and self-accusing. Beside him Coppinger began a spasmodic cough. The cough did not stop. It was too big for his shrunken body to contain and he seemed to be teetering on the edge of its convulsion. He realized that if Coppinger died there and then Ryan would know hardly anything about him. He thought that if he recovered he would question him about his family, his life, but as the cough subsided he felt the urge recede as though it were necessary to store an amount of blame.

'Away off and find your Captain X,' Coppinger said. 'You've me sick of looking at your big long face. Away on and find him and bury him if that's what you're looking. He hasn't got that long. There's no big friends looking after him now is what you hear. He's drawing too much attention down on too many people. Now it's in the open there'll be questions as to how he got away with it for so long. His own side'll set him up and get the other side to blow him away. Maybe the Brits will take him out. He's no fucking use to man or beast now.'

'What was he useful for ever?'

'You've no wit. Man like him keeps the pot boiling, keeps the fear going. Problem is now he's gone mad, no one can trust him. That's what I hear. I hear another thing too. You know your woman Heather? She's his woman. Here's us looking for Mr X all over the place and here's you at his woman all the time.'

Coppinger started to laugh then leaned forward and vomited on to the counter in front of him gently but insistently.

That evening Ryan went to see him at Belvoir Park hospital, which his father had referred to as the Fever Hospital. A name of last resort stored in the farther precincts of his mind; a name redolent of orphans and mothers dead in childbirth. But as he drove into the grounds Ryan found himself thinking instead of the well-tended suburbs on the outskirts of town that he had once longed for. It seemed that there was scope for dreaming in these approaches, an opportunity to enhance the way you thought about the ill, the tree-lined avenue offering hopeful, balanced living with all eventualities provided for.

He found the red-brick hospital buildings set among trees at the end of the avenue. There was the smell of cut grass and the sounds of a soccer match two fields away. Ryan got out of the car and leaned on the bonnet. Looking at the hospital grounds he had a sense of lost haunts. He remembered the beach chalets deserted at the end of the summer, their temporary interiors of warmed plank which seemed to become unmoored and drift knowingly from one season to the next. But when he went towards the cluster of hospital buildings he realized that they did not share this quality. He spent five minutes searching for an entrance before realizing that all the buildings faced inward, seeming abstracted, lost in troubled interior monologue.

Once he had entered the building it took even longer to find a nurse to direct him. This was male surgical, a forensic quiet in the corridors. Men in pyjamas looked at him incuriously. The mood was that of a camp for the displaced. There was exhaustion in the air which spoke of long nights, shortages, possessions shed. The men had a weatherbeaten look as if illness was a matter of climate.

Coppinger was sleeping alone in a small room at the far end of the hospital. His right arm which lay outside the bedclothes was connected to a drip. There was bruising around the entry point and Ryan felt as if he should remove it. It seemed to him that it was draining something essential from Coppinger's body. The plastic drip bag seemed to shiver, filling with a clear, other-worldly fluid. There was an empty cup beside the bed, scattered newspapers, a pair of glasses with one leg attached by tape, a transistor lying on its side. Signs of a ransack lacking in consequence. Coppinger's hands were bloodless, palms upturned, and his head lay awkwardly on four pillows. His sleeping body must have been left like that by the blue-uniformed orderlies Ryan had passed in the corridor, men who looked skilled in the inferences of mortality. Ryan found himself hoping that Coppinger would not die like that, in the position of a man caught unawares, prone to mischance. It could not be right. It was necessary to be more artful in the face of your own dying so that it did not come to you in a drugged hospital sleep arranged by nurses, your shallow breathing merely another element in an elaborate, tutored approach.

'He got a shot of morphine this afternoon.' Margaret was standing in the doorway. 'They said he complained of pain. It's good seeing him asleep, I think. He said he hasn't slept in months.'

She sat down carefully at the far side of the bed, looking down at Coppinger. Her hair was tied back and she wore no jewellery as though the situation demanded her plainness as a token of love.

'He just tipped forward on his face on the bar. At first I thought it was the drink.'

'I was just out of the bath when you rang. Another twenty minutes and I would have left the house.'

It was important to get each detail right. Where they were and what they were doing. Ryan closed his eyes to evoke the picture of her beside the bath with her head turned towards the telephone, a woman standing naked and ordinary just within the range of fearful news. It was an image which prompted a terrible carnality. In turn he was required to construct each scene in the bar for her. The spilled drink, the alert faces of bystanders, the proven strangeness of the day outside like any other day. They each felt the need of survivors to come together with tales of their own innocence. Then Margaret took one of Coppinger's hands in both hers and bent her head until it was resting on her fingers. Coppinger didn't stir but Ryan felt blame return like some old madness conceived in solitude.

He left them there. When he reached the car he found a piece of folded paper tucked under his windscreen wiper. He removed it and sat in the driver's seat. It was a sheet of paper torn from an exercise book. He opened it. It was signed by McClure and it read: THE END IS NIGH. This part was in capital letters. Across the bottom McClure had written a message in a gaunt derisive script. It read: Mr journalist I will try and get you an exclusive! PS I would advice staying away from Heather as she is his woman and that is danger.

Later that week Heather also heard from McClure. She was in the living room when she heard the sharp crack of the letterbox in the hall. She got to her feet, moving with difficulty. For several days she had suffered from a darkness in her mind and a creaking in the limbs and an ancient terror at night which would not relent. She did not draw back the curtains during the day and the house was beginning to deteriorate around her. There were bluebottles in the kitchen; a blurred murmur behind the door giving equilibrium to her days. She had not heard from Victor since the others had been arrested and thought that he must be on the run. She tried not to think of him abroad in the city, learning the ambiguous geography of the hunted and its evasive precepts. She wondered if he would come to her but realized that they could be watching the house. An unnamed surveillance seemed to emanate from the houses opposite and the trees on the pavement and the cars that were parked there day and night.

When she reached the hall she found a thick brown envelope which had been folded and pushed through the letterbox. She opened it and withdrew two sheafs of photographs. The first batch were part of a police line-up. These were recent shots of Big Ivan, Biffo and Willie, but it took her a moment to recognize them. Their faces were expressionless and she thought about stories Victor had recounted about Chinese brainwashing. The void gaze, dreamless. At the bottom was an older photograph of Victor. The smile he called gangster. She felt a stirring like a woman's plea on television for a missing son or husband.

The second batch came in an envelope which was marked Police: Evidence. The photographs here were like the ones that Darkie had once distributed, pathologists' colour prints. Yellowish cadavers laid out, naked and smoothfaced. She had read in a book that nothing erases wrinkles except death. Each body was bruised. Some had the neck severed and many were marked with knife-wounds on the torso and limbs, the marks regular, like the script of some phantom tongue used to record inventions that might be found on the lips of those about to die. Attached to each photograph was the pathologist's report detailing the injuries and the cause of death. Each had damage to the mouth or neck until it seemed to her that they had fallen under the rules of a curfew which required silence in perpetuity.

At the bottom of this pile was a typed charge sheet listing charges of murder against the men. At the end of this McClure had added Victor's name in his own handwriting. Victor Kelly! He was making sure that there was no doubt in her mind. She sat on the floor with the photographs spread around her feeling sure they contained a hidden imperative. She sat there for hours but could assign no meaning to them.

The next morning she dressed carefully, changing her usual make-up and wrapping a scarf around her head as a disguise. She called a taxi and waited for it sitting with a black patent handbag on her knees like a person called to attendance.

The taxi took her to the house that Willie Lambe had shared with his mother. When the old woman opened the door she looked Heather up and down, nodding her head slowly.

'You've gone to nothing,' she said. 'I've seen more meat on a butcher's apron.'

She stood back and allowed Heather to pass and stayed close to her as she entered and crossed the front parlour so that Heather had the impression of being conducted on a spectral tour through the old woman's unyielding remembrance. Heather was placed in a chair facing the window and the old woman sat with the light behind her again.

'I have surrendered William,' the old woman said venomously. 'He is without appeal in my heart. I told you before that I read a prediction of his crimes in the shape of his head the day and hour he was born. Of all the use that is put to a body a foul child is the worst.'

Heather had hoped that the woman had been to see her son, and that there might be news of Victor. But it had always proved a mistake on her part to put her trust in women. Particularly when it came to the desire of men when leniency was always beyond their reach. She realized that the only thing she would receive here would be a malice allotted to her for her part in Willie's life.

'When you come here first I says to myself, here comes a girl who will teach William devotion to his mother perhaps. Now he is gone for life it is a warning to me that a dirty woman will drag you to dirty places. I called the police myself this morning to offer helpful information on his habits and acquaintances and I described to them your name and purpose which is an unclean one.'

She reached for Heather's hand suddenly and placed it against her cheek.

'Here is the benefit of a good life in a fine skin. After eighty-six years forbye the worry of men.'

Heather pulled her hand away from the weightless lineaments of the old woman's pale skull. She felt her hand being grabbed again and she pushed her away, hearing her fall against one of the tables. She turned to run but felt herself momentarily frozen by the watchful eyes in the photographs of William's mother and it seemed to her that they were not the same person in each but many beautiful young women in their twenties, each with a wilful look which said they would not be overlooked, unnerved, or beguiled, and were capable of taking all that was given to them down to the last dark handful put to their unsurpassed lips.

'They're going to kill him,' the old woman hissed. 'It'd be a mercy to the world if you put a gun to his head yourself.'

twenty-two

McClure said to Victor to stay in the room above the Liverpool Stores in Sailortown until he could be certain that the others had not divulged his name under interrogation. He found himself in a dreamy mood and began to feel the return of the old foxy Victor, dressed to the nines with cash in the pocket, waiting in Maxies until some bored wife would smile at him with a warmth that told him she'd be grateful, or she'd show him her tongue unbeholden in the corner of her mouth, a present for Victor.

Holed-up. The phrase came back to him from the films. Holed-up in Sailortown. In the films it was an interval of promise. John Dillinger's late-summer thoughts in a wooden house on the edge of a forest while the lean-faced G-men searched elsewhere. He thought fondly of Heather, even if she betrayed him by accident under interrogation as women did; perilous words fell easily from their mouths.

McClure had arranged this room for him. It was one of the few houses left here, the buildings cleared to the water's edge, and the small store had been closed for years. He wandered through it at night holding the Browning pistol, confident in the irresolute dark of old workman's overalls, folded tea towels and damp-stained bolts of cloth. It was during one of these nights that he came across a man sleeping beside the broken window he had entered by. Victor lit a match and held the light on his face. The man's clothes and skin were encrusted with dirt and Victor recognized him as a man known as Smiley who would drink quietly in the doorways of Chichester Street until he reached the stage where he would begin to rage and growl like a dog, returning to the same spot every day as though bound to divest himself there of some ancestral madness. As Victor held the light over him his eyes opened and he regarded Victor calmly for a minute before he spoke.

'I know you,' he said. Victor studied him, unsure as to which form this knowing would take.

'I know you', Smiley said, 'for the bastard son of a bastard Catholic by the name of Kelly.' Victor raised the Browning and shot the man once in the stomach. Through that night he sat quietly beside him as he died. Neither of them spoke. Victor thought of that silence as being companionable. Smiley's breath was slow and considered in the knowledge that he would soon become accountable for each one and Victor wished him well with his breathing. He imagined that it was an old friend and comrade that was dying beside him and played with this far-off sorrow in his mind. He hoped that his was an opportune death and that he would fit the darkness prepared for him easily and without slippage.

It was only after dawn when he had disposed of the body in the coal bunker behind the house that he remembered the comment about his father. He found that he could not see his father's face in his mind. The meagre, pinched face looking worriedly about as if in constant danger of losing the thread of his own hopelessness. Or the look he reserved for his family, the gaze without properties designed to repel the most danger-ous thing in a dangerous world.

It was an imperfect time for a sense of loss. Water running from a cast-iron spout, wet spilled coal tracked across the yard, the mealy, unsettled light of dawn which seemed an exemplar of time spent in vain pursuit.

Victor spent most of his time in a room at the top of the house which looked out over the docks. He watched the channel buoys at night. Their alternate flicker, green—red, seemed faulty, short-circuited by some deep wildness in the tidal mass. Dorcas had warned him about the lough as a child; the sudden squalls, fast currents, sucking undertows. The sea to her was deadly and graceless — full of shifting bars and ancient murks that required a wariness beyond her comprehension.

During the day nothing stirred on the wasteland between the house and the water. Victor found that he could see faint outlines of the old streets on the ground. If he squinted his eyes he could almost see the streets themselves, windscoured and populous. The coopers on the quay, the ropeworks, the bakery, men selling milk from the tin, the honey-wagon from the abattoir. He thought about his parents meeting in an alley between the back-to-back houses, their two faces strange and animate.

But these were not his streets and he found himself drawn back to the night-time rides, with Willie Lambe driving, with few other cars on the streets and fewer people, and the sense that he had created a city-wide fear and put it in place and felt it necessary to patrol its boundaries.

He remembered how rarely the men they had lifted on these journeys had struggled or spoken. He prided himself on picking men who had a conviction of eventual solitude, natives of a wintry place. Smiley had been one, he realized, and he regretted that he had not brought a knife to work on him, to reveal the stony outlines of the silence within. It had been a mistake to hand over the task to Willie Lambe. Willie was a driver skilled in the tangible crafts of departure and destination. Willie kept his eyes fixed on the road oblivious to what lay beyond the verges; closed shopfronts giving way to fields with clouds in the dark east like wreckage gathered there.

There were rats in the house and Victor found a tin of Rodine Red Squill under the sink. He emptied half of the tin on to an old saucer, stirring the damp grains with his finger to bury the blue crystals of warfarin which were scattered on the surface like the leavings of some chemical malice. He placed the saucer beside a rat-hole and waited in the dark for one to appear, eat the bait and return to its den. He thought of a rat crouched wakeful through the night, suddenly redundant in its own world and alive to the exacting wonder of pain.

In the morning he found a skylight on the roof and climbed through it to find himself on the roof on the side which faced away from the water towards the city. A different territory now that he was looking at it from this height, seemingly unreliable with slithery, grey rooftops and the dominating bulk of the city hospital looking prone to moodiness, as if it were at any minute liable to become detached from its surroundings and begin a surly flotation seawards.

McClure had told him on the way that he had moved Heather from her own place to another house which was normally kept for meetings or interrogations. He imparted this information with the appearance of understanding that a woman's flesh is a fulsome commodity in times of trouble, and that he was making every effort to ensure her well-being. Thinking about this Victor was puzzled as to how McClure had persuaded him to come to this place which in daylight now seemed like a starkly lit setting for a hostage transfer or secret drug deal or some other exchange of bargains from a troubled world.

He remembered drinking in Maxies when McClure came in and took him aside.

'Pack your bags, son. Big Ivan's lifted. They got Willie and the knives and they pulled Biffo by the ears out of the Pot Luck an hour ago.'

Victor remembered going around the back of the bar for the Browning and tucking it into the front of his trousers. McClure reached out to him and pulled his shirt over it to conceal the butt. Outside there was a blue Escort at the kerb with its engine running. Victor had never seen the driver before and the man did not speak during the whole journey.

Victor realized that he had relinquished control in the bar with McClure acting iike somebody's uncle full of bluff assurance and awkward kindnesses. A hundred yards from Maxies they had been stopped at a police checkpoint which had Victor fingering the Browning and suffering from visionary images of policemen scattered dead or dying in the roadway, the face leaning through the car window shot away. He felt McClure's hand close over his. The driver took a wallet from his inside pocket and produced a plastic-coated card which he showed to the RUC man, then they were driving again.

'Ways and means, Victor,' McClure said, 'ways and means.' He settled back into his seat smiling as if the checkpoint had been a pleasurable interlude in an excursion which had its satisfactions neatly portioned.

'The way I see it, Victor,' he said after an interval. 'The way I see it is that you're a resource. Ulster needs men like you. Leaders. The struggle's going to be long and hard. The other three is the foot soldiers. They're done out. The point here is to get you out of harm's way for a while. Let things cool down.'

Victor looked out of the window. They were passing comfortable red-brick houses, their windows lit against early darkness and curtains as yet undrawn. For a moment he felt a pang of longing for the indistinct figures moving through their lit rooms, a dusk processional in the summoned warmth of their lives. These were the types of men that Victor had watched often as they left offices in the city centre carrying briefcases. The type of men he had despised then for being hurried, faintly shadowed, conditioned to sadness.

Twenty minutes later they were in Tomb Street. Victor saw a familiar figure on the pavement, moving close to the wall and casting furtive glances over his shoulder. A wino, he thought, lost in a wino's private melodrama. But as the car drew level he caught a glimpse of the face. Twisting in his seat he saw the man disappear into the doorway of the derelict Tomb Street bathhouse.

'Darkie Larche,' McClure said in a low threatening voice. 'Turned yellow so he did. There's a traitor for you. Would have shot you in the back, Victor, if he had the guts to do it.'

McClure was businesslike when they reached the safe house. Victor was in the grip of a bafflement which seemed to claim this place of empty spaces and deadly ocean glooms as its own. They sat silently in the back while the driver carried boxes of food from the boot of the car to the house. When he was finished McClure told Victor to stay indoors until word was sent that it was safe to leave. As they left Victor saw McClure laughing with the driver.

That last day in the house Victor stayed on the roof until evening. He felt clear-headed about his life now. He had seven thousand pounds buried under concrete in the back room of the Pot Luck, along with a sawn-off and five hundred rounds for the Browning. He had the black Capri. He had determination, a steely prerequisite to the outlaw life. From the films he knew that outlaws sometimes got lost in romance, and that it could become necessary to return to the basics of a savage, haunted existence. He could start by settling a score. When darkness fell he descended the ladder into the attic where he checked and loaded the Browning. In the bedroom he searched washstands and drawers until he found a rusted open razor. He left the house by the front door, his solitary figure retrieved by the spent landscape of the dock.

Heather had in fact moved, but McClure had not mentioned the raid. Sleeping in the front bedroom she had been awakened by the noise of a police radio outside; isolated voices and static like some grim wartime reportage. She looked at the alarm and saw it was 4 a.m. It seemed a fictional hour, derived from films she had seen, with wet streets, the sound of men's boots and pounding at the door. An hour packed with menace and grainy, dreamed happenings. Before she could reach the front door a soldier with a sledgehammer had knocked it off its hinges and within a minute there were soldiers and policemen in every room of the house. No one spoke to her, and if she had been asked afterwards to describe their faces she would have found it impossible. Their guns and uniforms expelled a cold smell of lonely hillside observation posts, isolated checkpoints. She sat at the bottom of the stairs. She had read about abducted children that day and thought this is what it would be like to be a parent of such a child — stricken helpless by an immobility in the heart. She could hear them shovelling coal from the coalhouse, lifting floorboards in the bedroom, emptying cupboards and drawers. A soldier came out of the bedroom carrying the microphone which had been on the wall behind the bed, its wire and metal gathered in his fist like the abstract cartilage and feathers of some dead thing lain undisturbed for years in the room's dust.

Shortly afterwards they left abruptly, leaving the house in disarray. Heather went around the house. There were holes in the floors and the contents of every cupboard were scattered on the floor. She was standing in the hallway still in her blue nylon nightdress when McClure arrived at eight o'clock.

'Fuck they fairly put the place over the body,' he said. He turned to her.

'Away and get your bits and bobs together. There's a house down the road where none of them'll touch hide nor hair.'

As she went up the stairs she saw him walking the corridor, hands clasped behind his back like a strange curator devoted to the artifacts of desolation.

At that time Dorcas was a woman beside herself with worry for a child. She was a mere fiend for news with the television on full all day besides the wireless and papers. Every time there was a report of a man shot or a body found with name withheld until next of kin were informed she felt the clutch of icy terror. These deaths were broadcast with only bare detail attached and she dreaded to find Victor among these sad facts. She did not know the best direction for her feeling. She sometimes implored that her son's name would come up as arrested at a scene and held for questioning. She could not remember the time lapsed since his last visit. She thought of him unattended somewhere in a gruelling pain of mind or body unable to call on her to perform a mother's office. In the end there was only one thing to be done. There were plenty of women to tell her the house where Victor saw the girl Heather. They would smile sweet as pie at Dorcas but with a viper concealed. It was common knowledge that the girl was there for any man that wanted.

She left the house early that morning in a bleak rain having taken special notice to her appearance and arranged for a taxi to call. She knew that the girl would take advantage from any breach of dignity such as wet hair or any failure in the apparel to impress. When the taxi pulled up outside she surveyed the house with the trained eye of a woman who has moved too often to be fooled by anything a house had to show. She was able to see a lack of care, a tenant who was unable to cope with landlords and estate agents or else was too busy in her noted career as a tramp.

It was only when she walked up the path though that she saw all was amiss. The front door was veered sideways on its hinges with the lock broken. The wits were put out of her and she ran forward with a worried cry before mastering her emotion. Taking her courage in both hands she pushed the door aside and entered the premises without further ado. Inside was a state of dissolution with everything tossed and holes dug in the floor. It was with an agony of apprehension that she explored every room thinking perhaps to find Victor dead and cold. She did not draw breath until she had made sure that this was not so.

It was only then that she sat up and took full heed of the situation. She could see it as a place left behind in a hurry like a tale of utmost desertion but it took the woman's eye to see the things vital to feminine behaviour removed. Even a woman mad for haste would not disdain what was necessary in the cosmetics line. Especially a woman like this whose face was a living and who would have all the trappings of a Jezebel. Sure enough in the bathroom there was a fortune in money of make-up which showed that the girl had her hand in Victor's pocket.

But Dorcas was able to see that essentials such as cleanser were gone which meant that she had left freely, perhaps with Victor.

She left the bathroom and went into the bedroom which was an offence with articles of clothing scattered and bed-sheets that had not seen the inside of a washing-machine for months. It made her cry to see this and recall her hopes of Victor. She would see him in her mind, him smiling beside a pretty girl, perhaps holding a child of his own to break his heart. Instead he was a desperate character on the run. Here was one mother who would not benefit from the entitlements of age. She sat on the bed and gave in to grief.

She could not say what time it was when she came to herself. The first thing she noticed was the cheap smell of the room like a degrading perfume. Her first act was to seek a mirror and straighten her hair. When she looked at the clock she saw that she had spent close to two hours in the house. The risk of discovery put the heart sideways in her. That woman surveying her with brazen eyes. The house was like a place in a time of desolation and it crossed her mind that the blame for destruction might be put on her shoulders like so much else. Panic seized her and she ran down the stairs and fled by way of the front door, going down the path like a woman with devils in pursuit.

She did not slow her pace until she got home. People looked strangely at her but she was blind in her senses. She reached the house and slammed the door behind her and stood in the hallway with the perspiration rolling off her. At that moment James came out of the living room and gave her a look of concern. He came towards her but she would not suffer him to touch her and lifted her hands to ward him and took herself upstairs and would not be consoled.

twenty-three

Ryan had never known of the existence of Tomb Street baths but now that he was beside it in the car it seemed the ominous heart of the city. A red-brick Victorian structure with fleshy sandstone abutments, the windows boarded and holes in the slate roof visible in the charnel glow of a street-light. A bathhouse for the industrial poor, gaslit, looming eerily out of a gaseous fog. A moody, imperfect place with fitful winds blowing debris against its bleak walls.

McClure had called him in the office just as he was about to leave. It was the hour of the shift change when there were few people in the building. There was a low hum of machinery, lights going out in offices across the street. Ryan tried to avoid the office during the change-over. It was a time to fall prey to a perilous nostalgia.

'Well, Mr Journalist,' McClure said, 'you ready for a bit of action?'

'What do you mean?'

'You want the story on our friend Victor? He's gone spare so he has, finally lost the rag. There's a few people in a high state of concern about his activities. Reckon he's got bad for business in the town. Word is he's going to be took out.'

'What are they going to do? Who's involved in this?'

'Hold your horses there, son. That's a bit down the road yet. First things first. By the way, I hear Coppinger's took bad. From what I hear the man's fucked.' Ryan said nothing. 'Suit yourself. Anyhow since you're the big journalist there's something I want you to take a look at. Say I'm giving you the exclusive. Tomb Street baths. If I was you I'd get my arse down there quick as I could. You wouldn't want to miss the scoop. Take a torch with you. There's a back door lying open. Nobody there to give you any problem if that's what you're worrying about. Safe as houses so it is.'

'What's the story?'

'Never you mind. Just get yourself down there.'

'What about Kelly?'

'I'll be in touch never you fear, Mr Journalist. Get on down to Tomb Street, there's a good lad.'

McClure hung up. Ryan felt light-headed, his hand trembling. A reckoning lay ahead and he was unsure as to its nature.

The previous day he had gone to the remand hearing for the other members of the Resurrection Men. The foyer of the courthouse was packed, clamorous with pressmen and relatives of the accused. Dry-eyed younger women and others who looked like they could be mothers – frail and noisome elders. There was a group of young men standing at the doorway, smoking and scanning the faces of lawyers and journalists with violent promise.

Inside the courtroom there was silence as the defendants were brought in. Ian Samuel Barnes with his head down. Ivan Robert Crommie smiling and waving to the public gallery with a lax foolish hand. William John Lambe also looking towards the public gallery, but fearfully, as if something there might quell him where he stood.

Charges of murder against the three were read by the clerk against which they entered pleas of not guilty. A police inspector gave evidence of their arrests and the confession of Crommie. He confirmed the murders, which had taken place over the previous four years, read the names of the victims and described the nature and extent of their injuries. When an application of bail was put forward he opposed it, stating that the leader and most dangerous member of the gang was believed to be still at liberty in the city although none of the defendants had named him, being in fear of their lives. Bail was refused.

Ryan studied them. He expected to see their crimes outlined there, some terrible detail of mouth or eyes. He expected faces of perceptible evil but they were ordinary. Glancing into the public gallery he saw Heather. She had lost more weight and the skin around her eyes was dark. He thought of the face of a condemned murderess, pale features glimpsed in a dramatic penal gloom.

As the three men were being led down to the cells Big Ivan raised a clenched fist in salute towards the public gallery. There was no response. They knew that he had broken and implicated the others. Big Ivan's eyes moved from face to face and each was averted in its turn. His lips moved as though naming the people and the streets they came from, as if their denial of him was geographic, pertaining to the parts of the city.

Outside relatives of the victims had gathered opposite the main gateway. Their faces were uncertain and strained, scarcely believing that nothing was required of them save this vigil. Ryan saw Heather coming towards him. She took his arm and he felt a reluctance to be touched by her.

'Victor found me,' she said urgently. 'He just turns up at the door the other night with the blood dripping off him. I think he must have killed someone again. He just sits there talking like he's not right in the head, how he's going to take over the town and all. My own head's away with it. Somebody's got to do something.'

'What do you want me to do?' The woman looked away from him towards the small group of relatives opposite the courthouse and her face softened as though she found consolation in their beleaguered stance.

'I don't know. I thought maybe with you in the papers and all.' She spoke vaguely now, her thought requisitioned.

'I don't know,' she repeated, 'the head lets you down

sometimes.' She turned abruptly and walked away from him with jerky steps. Ryan watched her cross the street, a halting and afflicted withdrawal.

On the way to Tomb Street he had bought a naggin of Powers whiskey. He had half-emptied it while driving and finished it now in two long swallows, feeling that the place he was now about to visit required some drift, the mind passive and inclined towards tolerance. He got out of the car and stood looking in the direction of the docks. A gull flew across the end of the street and wheeled urgently and then was gone as if driven by the wind to ratify the darkness beyond. Ryan switched on the torch and walked through the broken fence at the side of the building, moving the beam until he saw a steel-shuttered door propped open. He stepped inside and immediately the noise of the wind was reduced to a minor register, the complaint of a weird and ancient mania. He shone the torch down a long corridor. Its white walls seemed to phosphoresce and shimmer slightly as though something had remained unresolved in their construction. There was a familiarity about the place. Although he did not know what it was he felt a part of him lay claim to it. The torch beam found a door marked Office. He tried the handle but it was locked and it seemed to him that the place had fallen under a darker administration. Halfway along the corridor he discovered a smear of blood on the wall. He went on until the corridor turned sharply to the left where there were signs for the changing rooms and the baths. It was there that the smell first reached him, an aqueous bathhouse odour of Jeyes fluid, carbolic soap and a residue of the bare, chilled flesh of men filed through here in their thousands. Walking on he came to the changing rooms. There was horror here. Men cubicled naked or padding silently towards the baths. He remembered his father stripping wet swimming trunks and discarding them with a wet slap on the floor then towelling his head and neck vigorously. He was gaunt from the waist up, but his belly and fallen buttocks shook dreamily like filled panniers. He would turn and walk towards his folded clothes, his body seeming vast, abstract, burdened.

Ryan stepped through the shallow footbaths which would have contained warm, pink disinfectant. The light caught something lying there and he bent and saw that it was human skin, a bloodless medallion with the imprint of a shoe on it. He straightened and went on towards the bathhouse. He felt a crunch under his foot. The torch showed a piece of tooth enamel, its edge bevelled and stained with tobacco. Further on he found the whole tooth with the pink root attached like some strange anemone. He shone the torch upwards then and saw the vaulted brickwork roof of the bathhouse itself. The walls were made of white tiles with green tiles inset. The baths were porcelain with brass fittings and there was a stagnant briny odour which reminded him again of the seawater baths where his father had worked for four months one year and how he had clung to the man's neck while he swam the length of the pool, a tiny figure perched there, mute and fearful, as his father's body lurched over terrible depths. He lowered the torch and moved forward again, finding more blood and fragments of skin. Water dripped in the distance. Lying on top of old rags he found a severed finger gone white around the knuckle as though the man who owned it still held all his doings in the world in a wild grip. He felt that he could go no further but there was a second severed finger a foot away from the first and this one was crooked with the appearance of beckoning.

He found Darkie Larche naked in an empty bath. His torso was incised with small cuts meticulously executed and his head was bent to his chest as though there were something written there he could read, words in a severe tongue. Looking closer Ryan could see that the man's throat was cut and that his blood had run to the bottom of the bath and into the plughole, the whole scene composed like an anatomical plate devised for instruction with parts exposed and parts covered and rudimentary surgeons standing around looking lost to civilization.

In the week following the remand hearing for the other men Victor began to return to his old haunts, easing the Capri down side-streets, entering bars by the back door. Men greeted him cautiously. About you, Victor son. He never had to put his hand in his pocket for a drink. Barmen accepted that they were dealing with something outside the ordinary range of commerce and set drinks before him unasked. Victor sat alone at the bar and the other drinkers spoke in low confidential tones. The skin on his face had shrunk back on the bones and the men stole glances at him, sensing an erudition in the matter of last moments. They knew who he was and each thought of themselves alone with him in a deserted place. Each thought of himself becoming an exponent of the solitude within.

Victor kept newspaper cuttings about the Resurrection Men which he would spread out on the bar in front of him. The emphasis had begun to switch from the arrested men to their leader. They referred to a mystery man which pleased him. He saw himself as a figure in the shadows, someone elusive and dangerous to know. He thought that he could become a celebrity and give interviews to the papers on a regular basis. He imagined himself at parties, subject to admiration. He thought about expensively dressed women with small but immaculate breasts and voices that hinted at mannered raptures. He saw himself wearing a dinner jacket in well-lit rooms, prone to a little sorrow sometimes amidst the gaiety. Continuing his thought along these lines he realized that he was well rid of the others who lacked class. He congratulated himself on the way he had mentally seen the advantage arising from their loss.

Heather was another who had become a source of stress in his life. She had become a sloven in her personal appearance and would sit in the house sometimes crying fit to frighten the dogs in the street. He had told her about Darkie Larche and how he had screeched like a cut cat in the bathhouse, but then he realized that it was an error in judgement to give operational details to a woman. He had fucked her a few times for something to do but could not concentrate for the noises coming out of her. The spectral groans.

He gave attention to re-establishing himself after the setback of the arrests. The Larche job had served to announce his return as well as settling an old score, but more needed to be done. He realized that he had experienced a problem with clear thinking over some months so he obtained some speed from a man named McCaughey who kept it for greyhounds. He began to spend nights in the back room of the Pot Luck again, his head lost in chemical dazzle until the speed began to wear off with the advent of another glassy, Belfast dawn. At these times he started to think about his mother. He was reluctant to approach the house in case the police or even former members of Darkie's unit had it watched but it brought tears to his eyes to think of the hardness of her life. The last time he was home she had given him a photograph which showed her holding him as a baby while his father stood beside them looking away. Her eyes contained an earnest sorrow. Victor's eyes were sombre and watchful.

He would return to the house early in the morning and go to bed without speaking to Heather. She spent her day in the kitchen where she lit the oven and opened its door for warmth. Half-empty cans and milk cartons stood on the table. She sat by the oven smoking and running her tongue over her lips to taste the rancid, salty atmosphere of the warm room. She found a pile of *Reader's Digest* magazines under the stairs and read them at night when Victor was gone, looking for stories of a woman's survival against lonely odds. The story of Florence Nightingale. The story of Grace Darling. During those last weeks McClure began to ring her at night. First of all he would ask about Victor. Where was he now? What time did he leave? What was his state of mind? Was he confused? Elated?

Vanquished by memories? She did not know what to answer. He was a taste of old blood in her mouth. He was an entanglement in her heart.

Often McClure would begin to murmur obscenities down the line to her. Accounts of bondage, group sex, bestiality. She would lie against the wall holding the receiver to her ear and feeling afflicted with a sense of melancholy.

Sometimes the phone would ring and there would be no one on the other end but she would keep the instrument to her ear feeling calmed by its glacial hum.

She knew that it was a question of waiting for the end now. A woman could foretell these things when she was in a predicament of love. Though her heart had hardened when Victor had told her about Darkie. It would have been different if Victor had shot him. If he had been gunned down in a siege or an ambush and expired with a snarl on his lips and defiance for ever in his eyes.

She knew that Victor's time was near an end and for this reason she stayed in the house with him. She thought that the reason he had not been arrested was that another end awaited him. Her part was to wait. She thought that she might be asked to betray him. McClure was capable of it. But she would refuse. She had read of a woman spurned who betrays her man but it always ended up with no triumph but a bitter secret and then regret for life.

twenty-four

Ryan drove across the city to Margaret's, entering heavy traffic at Shaftsbury Square. He wondered if there was blood on his clothes. He was disoriented. It was Saturday night and he felt adrift in a scene from an era of commonplace cruelties. Men driving cars beside him looked masterful; their women looked around them with self-possessed eyes, displayed macabre lipstick. A police Land-Rover blocked the top of Sandy Row, back doors open on its foundry-made armour. An interior that the city had dreamed upon itself. Cold, functional, ghostly. The radio said there was a suspect vehicle in York Street, incendiaries in Lisburn.

Chlorine Gardens were quiet, shadowed. A place where graceful living with Margaret had seemed possible. Measured days. Standing on the doorstep he thought about the time when he had a wife and a marriage and how these words spoken had tonight acquired a deathly timbre.

As he followed her in his walk seemed unwieldy, newly learned. When he saw his face in the mirror it was full of calamity. In the living room she sat opposite him with her hands folded in her lap.

'Coppinger's dead,' she said suddenly. He stared at her. The familiar room seemed flooded with death.

'They called me from the hospital this afternoon. By the time I got there he was going. I was the only person there. I tried to get you at the office.'

'I left at the end of the shift.'

'He died without regaining consciousness. That's the way you say it, isn't it? I was holding his hand. I kept talking to him in case he could still hear me, saying his name. His breath just kept coming slower and getting shallower.'

Ryan summoned a picture. Coppinger dying with slow deliberation. Margaret conscious of her role as lone witness, reciting the bare text of his name. He crossed the floor and knelt in front of her, holding her hands.

'Did he say anything at all?'

'Before that he did. He says dead quiet to himself, "I'm sorry."'

As though to die were not quite a crime but a misdemeanour subject to penalty and forfeit in a small way. She put her arms around his neck and wept as if she also had amends to make.

He stayed in the house for the two days before the funeral. Darkie's body was discovered on the first day but he said nothing to her regarding the encounter in the bathhouse. They spoke softly to each other and steered clear of reminiscence about themselves. They brought up details about encounters with Coppinger, marginal incidents, and sat silent afterwards. She went to bed early while he sat in front of the television with the volume low and the lights turned down. In the early hours of the morning the house acquired a dim, monastic atmosphere. He noticed that she had made new curtains, added shelves beside the fireplace. Addressing herself to what was needful in her life. He recalled the things that Coppinger had concerned himself with. Informers. Vivid assassins. Dark legatees of the city's will. When Ryan had been leaving the office after his first day at work Coppinger had shouted at him. Hey you, cuntyhole, what's your name? Taking him from bar to bar. The Crescent, the Eglantine, Kelly's Cellars, Muldoons, Rocktown. The company of old men repeating tales of the shipyard and the Blitz; far-off salutary talk of the aged. Pre-arranged encounters with groups of men in back rooms. Men from the Markets, men from the Short Strand, Sandy Row, detectives from Castlereagh. Drinking Black Label, Double Diamond, Black Bush, Jameson and red. Ryan would sit at the edge of the group and be unable to hear what they were saying. They had a way of cutting short their voices so that they seemed perpetually out of earshot. Late at night they seemed like men facing into a catastrophic gale which carried their voices and left them gesturing and grimacing.

When he told Margaret about this she said no. She pictured these meetings as an historical conspiracy, doomed to failure. Men with pale, strained faces, lamplit. But for all that, she said, Coppinger was a dirty old bastard too who never changed his shirt.

When she had been leaving the hospital a nurse had handed her a plastic bag containing his personal effects. There was a set of keys. He had lived in Sunnyside Street off the Ormeau Road, she told him.

The morning before the funeral they drove across the river to the house. It was part of a red-brick terrace on the narrow street. There were loyalist slogans on the walls. A wind came off the river and seabirds wheeled where they had been blown off course and their calling seemed to Ryan the preparatory notes to an advancing disaster. He found Margaret strange in her insistence on the visit. She was distant, precise in her movements. It seemed that she had practised this journey and each movement was an observed detail in an interior rite.

They did not speak when they were inside the house. It was what Ryan had expected. Dust everywhere, clothing piled on chairs, newspapers, empty bottles. On a shelf there was a street directory of the city published sixty years before listing the occupants of each street and their positions. He picked it up and ran a finger down one column. Riga Street: home to a brewer, a cobbler, a spinster. There were no other books, and

Ryan imagined Coppinger bent over this one as if the lamentation of the city was encrypted in its narration of street-names
and dead inhabitants and lost occupations.

When he looked up Margaret was standing by the fireplace
with a framed photograph in her hand. He went over and took
it from her and knew at once that it showed Coppinger and his
father. The photograph was old, the emulsion beginning to
blacken and disintegrate but the two figures were plainly
visible. The man was elderly. He had the austere look of those
who have children late in life, a look of having laboured to the
point of fatherhood, and there was a severity in the way he laid
his hand on the boy's shoulder, an unwillingness to cede
anything other than that labour to his son. The boy was looking
up at his father and Ryan recognized the fear in his eyes and
the child's fatal knowledge that his father would never be
anything more than a figment. When they were leaving Margaret wanted to take the photograph. He said sorry, she said.
But Ryan took it and placed it on the fireplace and consigned
the child and the man to the company of their unforgiving
forebears.

It was McClure who brought Victor the news about James.
Victor was in his place at the corner of the bar in the Pot Luck
when McClure sat down beside him. There was racing on the
television. Chepstow, Aintree. Overcast scenes. The going
heavy and the commentator's voice laden with universal sadness and darkness coming early.

'Cunt,' Victor said without turning his head. 'You would of
left me lying down there in that friggin' house.'

'Nothing I could of done about it Victor, peelers all round
the place. If I'd of moved I would of took them right to you.'
There was reproach in McClure's voice. Friendship doubted.

'Any word of the boys?'

'Don't worry your head about them. They're took care of.

Big Ivan's happy as a pig in shit acting the sectarian killer. Word has it Willie's turned good living. Him and God's like that these days. Biffo's the same as ever. The boys is took care of Victor. That's not what I'm here for.'

'You're always here for something anyhow. Listen, McClure, the town's gone to shit so it has. IRA bastards run mad. Every time you turn on the telly there's some politician talking the mouth off himself, dose of their own medicine's what they want. But I'm telling you our lot won't lie down for ever. Got to light their fuse for them though. All we need is more guns. I got a list of guns to give you. I got a list. I got it here in my head.'

'Just take it easy there, Victor. Time enough for all that. I ·got a message for you. Your ma's been doing the nut looking for you.'

McClure was now the friend in times of crisis.

'Your da's went and took a stroke. He's in a bad way. Can't move nor nothing. They had him in the Royal but he's home now.'

'Look,' Victor said, turning his head so that he was looking directly into McClure's face, 'do you see a tear in them eyes?'

'Fuck's sake, Victor, blood's thicker than water. Besides your ma's going mental. Families is hard I'll grant you that. But are you going to sit here with your arse picking buttons and your ma going mad with worry about you?'

'No room for traitors. Man standing idly by. Men shedding their blood, he's up to the neck in pigeon shit.'

'It's the ma, Victor. Just the one visit. There's no peelers watching the house or nothing. I'll drive you up and wait for you. Five minutes is all. I'll be outside. After we'll go for a drink. There's some boys I want you to meet. High-ups. Heard all about you so they have. Admiration for a man who's strong on principle, not afraid to get the hands dirty. Get that drink down your neck there and come on.'

'I have it all in the head, McClure. Names, dates, places.

Turn this town inside out. They haven't heard the last. Hands in pockets in this town. I know the type of them. They haven't heard the last of me.'

McClure drove Victor towards the house and Victor sat silent while the other man recited incidents that Victor had instigated or been party to. He mentioned his victims and the places they had died. One after the other until it seemed to Victor that he had produced an itinerary to accompany a journey through a trackless region whose borders were disputed between the living and the dead.

It was a short drive but it seemed long to Victor. He looked for faces he knew among those entering and leaving the pale-lit vestibules of shops along the road but some impedance lay between him and them, and the place-names which McClure continued to enumerate seemed part of a strange other topography, surveyed and mapped and returned to silence. The tone of McClure's voice altered and he began to speak of different things. Good times, Victor. Victor dressed to the last, women chewing the tongue off themselves for it. Always two or three of them hanging out of you and their husbands tripping over their own two feet to set a drink in front of you. Days of plenty. Walk into any shop and clean out the till and your man standing there with a smile hanging off his ears fit to choke him saying, anything else I can do for you, don't hesitate, Mr Kelly. Victor knew the moves. Parked up at the bar of the Pot Luck with the rest of them at night with the barlights dimmed, all drunk and admiring their own past deeds and poolballs that clicked soft and gradual and the men at the bar calling bets in low, serious voices and watching every ball as though absolution itself was staked on the outcome.

He did not mention a figure kneeling on wet ground held by one man while another bent over him engaged in an intricate task, the whole composition defined by a car's headlights.

When they reached the house McClure stopped and Victor got out without a word and crossed the pavement without looking back. McClure drove the car to the end of the street and turned it because he wanted a good vantage point for what was to follow. He saw everything was as it should be. Cars parked each to its house and women coming home from shopping and a group of children swinging from a rope tied to a lamppost turning this way and that, testimony to men hanged and sundry baleful transactions for vengeance carried out under a lowering sky.

Dorcas knew the day James took ill that she was indeed a woman born to misfortune. A ring came to the door at lunch-time and she was not in error to feel dread at the unexpected visit. She went to the door in a state of collapse to be told by a neighbour that James had taken a turn and had gone to the Royal in an ambulance with blue lights. She went swiftly upstairs to the hot press for necessities she kept prepared there, such as new pyjamas and underwear still in the cellophane so that when she got to the hospital there would be no nurse looking down her long beak on old worn things.

The week James spent in hospital passed for her like a dream of attendance among the sick. When she spoke to doctors she used her husband's full name, Mr Kelly, to show them here was a woman proud of standards. She was told there was a loss of oxygen to the brain resulting in an impairment of facilities. Walking, arm movement, speech. Impairment of facilities she thought and closed her mind to the fearful word paralysis.

At the end of the week James was taken home in a wheelchair. Not a word had passed his lips in the full time. Then it sank in that to cater for an invalid was to be her bitter lot. To change and feed and wipe spittle from a thankless mouth. She thought sometimes that this stroke was a thing he done to break her. He did not look at her and there was no smile or any badge of remorse. He sat in the chair as if tied to it like a hostage in an ordeal. Looking on him she felt despair claw at her that she was now no more than a servant. A family by another name would have had neighbours around to render sympathy but the old song of having a Catholic name had surfaced and this was a neighbourhood of Catholics out. All the time she was in a desperation for Victor to come home. She thought of herself talking to him at the kitchen table and how he would use words admiringly to her or show love in a glance of sympathy.

She thought then that Victor was ashamed of coming home because of his friends in prison and determined to get a message to him that no blame attached. She knew that the Pot Luck had formerly been a favourite with him for pool and watching horses on television and a message might find him there. She thought of herself like a mother's story in a magazine of a dogged hunt through an uncaring world but in the end victorious. It was in this mind that she found herself at the front door of the Pot Luck with her hand on the latch and her nerves jumping. When she opened the door it was almost with relief that Victor was not there. Instead there were two men playing at pool and one man on his own sitting at the bar. She crossed the floor with dignity but heard one of the men at the pool table say, fuck me, it's the queen herself come to visit. She stood in front of the bar until the barman came up to her and said, what can I get for you, your majesty? She cut him with a look to say that here was a woman who was not in the habit of frequenting public bars, then said it straight out that she wished to speak to Mr Victor Kelly. At which point the barman took on a nervous disposition and licked his lips until she wondered if he was simple in the head. It was with a feeling of gratitude that she turned when the man beside her spoke up, saying excuse me but would you be Mrs Dorcas Kelly? It was a correct way of speaking like a man in an office to give you confidence. He had brown eyes and a look like he was kind but weary at the sadness in the world.

She said yes, she was Victor's mother, and needed to get in contact urgent with him as a result of a family matter. He said he understood and he had heard about her misfortune. He said that his name was Billy McClure, that an unexpected illness was often a shock to the system and that family was a comfort in time of trouble. Dorcas found herself glad that Victor had a friend with respect for the family. Here was someone to whom she could produce her troubles and know that they would not be a cause of vulgar laughter like from the other two at the pool table.

She asked him straight did he know where she could find Victor. He said that Victor moved often due to the dangers for a man prominent and respected in the city but that he could get a message to him. He asked when Dorcas wanted to see him and she said heartfelt as soon as possible. He said would the next day be all right and she said yes.

At home that night she felt better in herself than she had in weeks. There was a lightness in her head as of a burden lifted. And when she looked in the paper to see that there was football on, which she hated, she still turned on the set for James to see although there was no sign of gratitude from that quarter. But if she had known what the next day had in store she would not have entertained glad thoughts and she often recalled Billy McClure's final words that soon she would always be able to find Victor when she wanted him.

Dorcas was preparing to shave James when Victor arrived. She had a bowl of hot water and a safety razor on the coffee table and had a towel around his neck so that he looked like someone prepared for surgery. When she heard the front door open and close she knew that it was Victor and it seemed that James also knew because he twisted his head and made a noise in his throat like a sound taken from the extremity of human expression. She turned to the door as it opened but the words of welcome died in her mouth. At first she thought it was not him in the doorway, he was so thin and pale, and James made the noise in his throat again as if he looked upon some cadaverous visitant come to claim his soul. She saw that Victor's leather jacket was torn and that his jeans were dirty. He looked like a man newly come from unspeakable disaster. His face was haggard and his eyes were without expression as he looked upon his parents so that Dorcas felt herself as if on trial for some great crime she knew not what. I was about to shave him, she said, gesturing towards James. Your father, she said. Victor turned towards him with calm surmise. He had not spoken yet. Your father can wait, she said, I'll get you some food. You look like you haven't ate in days. You're like a rake, she said. I'll do it, Victor said. He spoke slowly as though words were alien to him. I'll shave him, he said.

It occurred to Dorcas to ask Victor where he had been and what had befallen him there as he gave the appearance of a man in the last throes of distress. But she did not ask.

Victor lifted the shaving bowl and approached his father with it. He started to soap his jowls and upper lip, covering them lavishly with the soap as if this were a thing he wished to efface utterly, banish to some starless littoral the mildly wattled flesh. Above the lather the dark eyes stared back at him devoid of the precedents of fatherhood. Victor soaped until the foam was smooth and bland then replaced the brush and lifted the small metal razor, testing the edge of it with his thumb and dipping it once into the bowl of hot water. He gripped the angle of his father's jaw with his left hand and tilted it backwards, his red eyes glistening and a smile on his face like an idolatrous barber. He continued to force his head back until the neck was painfully stretched and his eyes stared towards the ceiling and it seemed to Dorcas that the look was cold and unreckonable. With the left hand that supported his father's jaw Victor began to probe beneath the lather, touching the neck sinews, the windpipe, the carotid artery, as though there was something instructive in the anatomy itself, an atavistic revelation beneath the surface of the skin. He dipped the razor again into the bowl of light and examined the blade and the fine peripheral light along the edge. Dorcas thought that this was not like a man shaving his ill father. Victor began to shave with long strokes, working upwards from the thorax and she saw him pull the skin sideways from the Adam's apple that only a man has. Victor shaving the cheeks now, a small smile on his face as if hasty words concerning his father had never crossed his lips. Women fetch and carry, she thought, and their hearts lie to them. With the heel of his left hand under James's chin Victor shaved the top lip then threw the razor down on the table. He released his father's jaw so that it fell forward on his chest. James lifted his eyes slowly to meet his son's gaze then flinched and turned away.

'That's you done, da,' Victor said softly.

'That's a great job, son,' Dorcas said. 'I always cut the face off him. Take's a man.'

'I finished him and I got to go now.'

'You only just walked in the door.'

'Still and all ma there's things I got to do. I've this meeting arranged with these influential men. I can't tell you about it.'

'Would you not stay for a drop of tea, son? I know by your da that he's glad to see you.'

'Do you reckon, ma? But the da knows all the vital things I done for Ulster. He's got a pile of articles cut out of the paper and all, isn't that a fact, da?'

Dorcas looked surprised at James. A man who never took an interest. A man who would not walk the length of himself to accompany his son to juvenile court. James met her eyes and made a low sad sound and she said to herself yes, well may you regret wasted time now when your son is mingling with leading figures in the community and you are silent as if struck down dumb for punishment.

She stood with her hands joined in front of her like a mourning figure as Victor walked towards the door. 'Come back soon, son,' she said. He turned at the door and smiled at her. He made his hand into the shape of a gun the way he used to.

Any funny business and you get this, doll, he said in an American gangster voice. That was all until she heard the shots outside.

Coppinger's funeral was poorly attended. There were some neighbours from Sunnyside Street and a deputy editor from the paper who avoided Ryan. Two of the gravediggers had to help carry the coffin. It seemed a pauper's funeral, shameful and mean. Margaret wore a hat with a small veil attached. She looked small and ageless and the clergyman deferred to her. It was a dark afternoon, still, and there was low cloud over the mountains. A day for the Resurrection Men. A day which bespoke the night to come and men carrying hooded lanterns and a long clanking journey by cart and ship's hold to the slabs of the dissectors. The four men lowered the coffin into the grave then stood back with hands joined. The priest opened his prayerbook and he looked towards them and began his plain instruction as to the routes taken by the dead and the destinations of their souls.

Afterwards Margaret suggested that they go to the Crescent bar. She directed him through manifold small streets until he was lost. Battenburg Street, Cupar Street. Burnt-out streets, divided streets, memorial streets. As though she could sleuth Coppinger's path through them, a tract of his passing written from house to pub to intersection. Ryan did not interfere although it was almost night, if night described the fraught blackness closing from the mountains and the freezing lough like the first coming of another governance of light which was infallible and cold. Eventually they turned a corner on to Sandy Row and he saw the Crescent. She parked the car outside and they went in. Margaret also had spoken little and now she sat silently at the bar while he ordered drinks. It was the first time they had been in a bar together since they had separated. He knew why they had come here. When all else had fallen away marriage was most unyielding in matters of death. He tried to summon Coppinger's face and felt instead a sense of damaged romance. He could not look at his wife beside him without the pain of transgression. There were a few drinkers sitting quietly in various parts of the bar as though each occupied a space allotted to them and it was a case of doing your best within those limits. A man came through the door and walked up to the bar.

'Shooting up the road,' he said.

'Who is it?' the barman said quietly.

'Word is it's Victor Kelly. Lying shot dead outside his ma's house.'

Margaret saw Ryan's expression.

'You know him?' He didn't answer. She jerked her head towards the door.

'Go on.' She dismissed him. Accustomed to men's disappointed trajectories.

'Pro job they say,' the man at the bar went on. 'Three of them. Fucking bang bang.'

Ryan turned briefly at the door but she was looking the other way.

McClure watched the blocking car pull out of its space which was then occupied by the van. It was a blue Commer with sliding cab doors. Bought from the Lilliput laundry or the bakery and roughly resprayed.

Victor didn't see it as he pulled the door closed behind him. He thought with satisfaction about the look in his father's eyes as he was being shaved. The razor was good but he would have to get another knife. He smiled at the idea of Willie's knives being produced in court, a charismatic weight all slither and hiss in a cellophane evidence bag. He thought about putting a knife into James's hand, his father's face a dream of obedience. He recollected his mother's reaction with warmth when he had said any funny business, and how he called her doll. Then he realized that McClure wasn't there and he felt an expression cross his face like in a film, something's wrong. His eyes searched the street and somehow he knew that it was a fateful wrong. He shaded his eyes and looked into the momentous dark. It was hard to see. He needed light, any light and there it was suddenly above him. A sniper's lonely moon. He saw the three men getting out of the back of the Commer van, running, carrying rifles held across their chests. He saw them take cover behind parked cars, raise the rifles into firing position. Victor had never thought it would be like this, time going by with deadly ease. He pulled the Browning out from under his jacket and looked for cover. But nothing was right. He wanted them to be serious-minded men who shouted out a warning. He wanted words full of allure and danger to shout back. Never take me alive. The rifle fire had a flat industrial sound. Victor felt the bullets force him back against the door. Victor knew the moves. Struggle to raise the gun. Clutch the breast and lean forward in anguish. His face hit the pavement. He did not see one of the men leave cover and walk over to him and put his foot in his neck and shoot him through the back of the head with a snub-nose revolver. There were no words, got him at last. No last rueful gangster smile, goodbye world.

twenty-five

The Harland and Wolff cranes are visible from everywhere in the city. Scaffolding abandoned from the beginnings of the world. A helicopter moved across the city with a searchlight picking out threadbare taxi companies and shops shuttered as though in the aftermath of looting. Each lit area noted for its history of riot, pogrom, act of reprisal. The Brickfields. Smithfield. The beam illuminated Heather at the bedroom window of the house in the Village and she watched the helicopter until it had moved on; poised on a buoyant mile of light which reminded her of the lights erected by a television crew at the scene of the shooting. An unearthly magnesium flare that made the faces of those standing around take on the pallor of exhaustion; fleshy women standing in doorways, policemen casting legendary shadows. She had not been allowed past the incident tape. In the distance she could see soldiers standing beside a Land-Rover. Victor's body lay on the pavement, his face turned away. His jacket was pulled up exposing his back so that she wanted to pull it down for him.

Later that night when she turned on the television news she felt as if she was watching something old-fashioned. Archive footage of an eerie killing; a slum murder, or somebody famous found dead in a mystery shooting. The camera found bullet marks, ejected cartridges ringed with chalk, moved to show people standing behind barriers. Among them she saw McClure, standing slighty apart with a custodial expression on his face which told her that this was his: the ambulance, the soldiers, the bystanders, Victor's outflung arm, these moody and choreographed night scenes. It was a staged murder, a minor spectacle with themes and digressions. No one had claimed the killing. A commentator hinted darkly that it was the work of a special unit within the police or army. Victor was described as a leading member of a notorious cutthroat gang. She knew that McClure would be feeding them information, outlining a plot. She imagined the enthralled conversations of men in pubs. Who shot Victor? Caught up in McClure's hypnotic fictions. She saw the journalist Ryan standing behind the tape with other onlookers. Among the midwinter faces. She thought he looked like a man invested with the bare details of his own end. She found herself waiting for Victor's Capri to pull into the street. The low sound of its engine, coming without lights, the assassin's dark and gleaming paintwork.

The Village 4 a.m. A steel road bridge built through the middle of the houses so that the bedroom windows were level with the top girders. Underneath the arches were full of small shops, coachbuilders, car seat upholsterers. A scrapyard sign promised cash for your old gas cooker, your old lead, the roof above your head, the ground beneath your feet. Cars along the road were stalled in beams of transit. Hairtrigger time. Heather woke with the feeling that Victor had been leaning over her, examining her face as though it were a map of consequences. She thought about an interrogator in a room with a plain table and a single bulb, edging one step closer to a complex and personal truth.

Ryan came to see her two days later. He said that he was on his way to the City Hospital. She was packing. Ryan was drunk. He looked as if he had been drunk for days. He moved like a strange amputee whose limbs did not fit him. Red veins crossed the vitreous whites of his eyes. She barely understood him when he spoke. He said that his father was a swimmer. He said that he was a shifty and felonious man. He talked about his wife. How men talk about their wives, she thought. Those lonely words. He told her that he had beaten his wife. He wept and she felt his desire that they should plead for each other as accomplices to events in the city. She knew that he wanted comfort from her but she could not give it as she had none left and no expectation of it again.

He said that he had been to see Victor's mother. She told him how she had knelt beside her son's body in the street until the police had arrived. How a soldier had taken her by the arm and led her back towards the house while men in white overalls had fallen to measuring and photographing as though they were seeking a geometry there on the ground from which they could calculate the parameters of a life and in some way replenish it. When they had finished they lifted the body on to a stretcher and carried it to an ambulance. Where are they taking him? Dorcas had asked. No one answered her. As the stretcher was put into the ambulance she saw polished instruments and tubes and it seemed that Victor had been recalled as surety in some bargain of flesh and metal. Where are they taking him? She asked again without reply. Ryan had talked with her through the evening until the light failed and she sat where he left her in the unlit house whimpering and crying like a child, offspring to the grisly night.

When he had told Heather this Ryan turned and walked away. She watched him until he reached the corner of the street. He was of the city now, part of its rank, allusive narrative, but she felt like a character in a strange tale. An outlandish woman. He was going, he had said, to the morgue in the City Hospital to see what the autopsy revealed, although they both knew what he would find. Bodies laid out as if for journey. That they would carry news of the city and its environs. The Pound. Sailortown. The Bone. That their news would be awaited. That they would test their quality against the dark and take their place among the lonely and vigilant dead.